DRESSING THE PAST

DRESSING THE PAST

Edited by
Margarita Gleba, Cherine Munkholt
and Marie-Louise Nosch

Oxbow Books

ANCIENT TEXTILES SERIES VOL. 3

Published by
Oxbow Books, Oxford, UK

ISBN 978-1-84217-269-8

A CIP record of this book is available from the British Library

This book is available direct from

Oxbow Books, Oxford, UK
(Phone: 01865-241249; Fax: 01865-794449)

and

The David Brown Book Company
PO Box 511, Oakville, CT 06779, USA
(Phone: 860-945-9329; Fax: 860-945-9468)

or from our website
www.oxbowbooks.com

Cover designed by Marianne Bloch Hansen.

Ancient Textiles Series Editorial Committee:
Eva Andersson, Margarita Gleba, Ulla Mannering
and Marie-Louise Nosch

Printed in Great Britain by
Information Press, Eynsham, Oxfordshire

CONTENTS

LIST OF ILLUSTRATIONS

LIST OF CONTRIBUTORS

Eva B. Andersson. Archaeologist specialized in North European archaeology. She received her Ph.D. from the University of Lund (Sweden). Her special area of study is textile production during the Iron and Viking Ages in Scandinavia. She is a project manager at the Danish National Foundation's Centre for Textile Research at the University of Copenhagen.

Cecilia Aneer. Teaches dress history at undergraduate courses in textile history. At present she is preparing for her Ph.D. in Textile Studies at Uppsala University, Sweden. Her research is in the field of tailoring techniques and clothing manufacture with a special interest in the Renaissance and Baroque periods.

Annette Borrell. M.A. in Media Studies from the University of Southern Denmark. She is the Administrative Officer at the Danish National Research Foundation's Centre for Textile Research at Copenhagen University. She is interested in film and costume and has lectured on the subject.

Margarita Gleba. Archaeologist specialized in pre-Roman Italian archaeology. She has worked on excavations in Italy, Turkey and Ukraine. She received her Ph.D. from Bryn Mawr College (USA). She is a project manager and postdoctoral research fellow at the Centre for Textile Research, University of Copenhagen, Denmark. Her special area of study is the archaeology of textile production.

Ilona Hendzsel. Textile designer and teacher of design, graduated from Moholy-Nagy University of Art and Design, Budapest, Hungary. She teaches textile design at Zichy Mihály Secondary School of Applied Arts, Kaposvár and works as a designer and producer of home fabrics.

Eszter Istvánovits. Történelemtudományok kandidátusa (Ph.D. Hungarian Academy of Sciences, Budapest). She is archaeologist and scientific secretary at the Jósa András Museum (Nyíregyháza, Szabolcs-Szatmár-Bereg County, Hungary). Her main fields of research are the Barbarians of the Roman Age in the Carpathian Basin, Early Migration Period and archaeology of the Upper Tisza Region.

Valéria Kulcsár. Történelemtudományok kandidátusa (Ph.D. Hungarian Academy of Sciences). She is an archaeologist at the Petőfi Museum (Aszód, Pest County, Hungary). Her main fields of research are Barbarians of the Roman Age in the Carpathian Basin, Early Migration Period, and rescue archaeology.

Helle Leilund. Candidata philosophiae (Copenhagen University) in European Ethnology and is curator at The National Museum of Denmark's Department for Modern Danish History. She is currently writing her Ph.D. thesis on how different people practise dress codes, uniforms and uniformity at work today. This project is undertaken within the context of the dress collection at the National Museum of Denmark.

Dorottya Ligeti. Assistant Professor at the Department of Leather Design at Moholy-Nagy University of Art and Design, Budapest. She graduated as a leather and fashion accessory designer from the Department of Textile Design at the same university and is at present preparing for her doctorate there. Her special area of interest is the possibilities for European footwear production in relation to competition from Far East Asian mass production.

Ulla Mannering. Archaeologist specialized in North European prehistoric and Roman textiles and costumes. She has also worked with the use and production of prehistoric plant fibre materials, especially nettle and flax. She received her Ph.D. from the University of Copenhagen. She is a project manager at the Danish National Foundation's Centre for Textile Research at the University of Copenhagen.

Tove Engelhardt Mathiassen. Candidata philosophiae (Århus University, Denmark) in Ethnography and Social Anthropology. She is Curator at *Den Gamle By* (The Old Town), National Open Air Museum of Urban History, Århus. A weaving teacher by profession, she has published articles on historical dress and textiles. Exhibitions: Bride and Groom – weddings and wedding outfits during 250 years (2004); Maternity Clothing (2005); Christening Robes (2006).

Cherine Munkholt. M.A. in History (University of Copenhagen); M.A. in Area Studies from the School of Oriental and African Studies (London University) and B.Soc.Sc. in International Studies (Birmingham University). She has worked as a freelance proof-reader since 1984.

Marie-Louise B. Nosch. Director of the Danish National Foundation's Centre for Textile Research at the University of Copenhagen. She is trained in ancient history and Philology. She has been educated at universities in France, Italy and Germany, and received her Ph.D. from the University of Salzburg. Her main research area is Bronze Age Mediterranean textile production, and in particular the Linear B inscriptions on Mycenaean textile production.

Anna Nørgaard. Professionally educated weaver and handicrafts teacher. She has lectured on and worked with reconstructions of prehistoric textiles for 25 years, and has exhibited her work at the National Museum of Denmark in Copenhagen, the University of Oslo's Antiquities Collection in Norway, and the Hochdorf Museum in Germany for its permanent exhibition on *Der Keltenfürst von Hochdorf*. She is specialized in weaving on a warp-weighted loom, and at present works at the Viking Ship Museum in Roskilde, Denmark where she is weaving a reconstruction of a woollen sail.

Andrea Óvari. A woven material and model designer and teacher graduated from the Textile Design Department at Moholy-Nagy University of Art and Design, Budapest. She is the managing designer of a Hungarian women's wear company and a teacher of costume history and drawing at the Model and Fashion School, Budapest.

Judit Pásztókai-Szeőke. Archaeologist specialized in Roman provincial archaeology. She is studying for her Ph.D. at the Department of Classics at Århus University and at the Danish National Foundation's Centre for Textile Research, University of Copenhagen. Her special field of research is textile production in the Roman province of *Pannonia* (present day Central Europe).

Maj Ringgaard. Textile conservator at the National Museum of Denmark who has lectured extensively in Scandinavia on textile conservation. She is studying for her Ph.D. at the National Museum of Denmark and at the Danish National Foundation's Centre for Textile Research, University of Copenhagen. She is a trained teacher in tailoring, weaving, knitting and needlecraft and studied archaeology before obtaining her M.Sc. in Conservation from the Royal Danish Academy of Fine Arts. Her main interests are historical textile materials and techniques.

Kathrine Vestergaard Pedersen. Candidata magisterii (Copenhagen University) in medieval archaeology and textile science is Activity Coordinator at *Hjemsted Oldtidspark* Iron Age Open Air Museum. She is interested in the development of the construction of garments, dress patterns and fabrics in the Nordic Viking and Middle Ages, with a special emphasis on combining theoretical analysis with practical knowledge garnered from handicraft processes.

ACKNOWLEDGEMENTS

This anthology received generous support from the Lillian and Dan Fink Foundation.

The following people deserve our special thanks: Peder Dam for maps; Agnete Wisti Lassen, who made the Timeline, helped with the illustrations and made useful suggestions; Annette Borrell and Ylva Cederborg who worked with the illustrations and helped with innumerable tasks in the final hectic weeks; Kitt Boding-Jensen who advised on illustrations in the early days of the project; Lise Bender Jørgensen, CTR's Visiting Professor who was always ready with inspirational comments and advice on different aspects of the project, and who patiently answered all questions; Anna Nørgaard, Ulla Isabel Mach-Zagal, Linda Mårtensson, Marianne Bloch Hansen, Inge Kjeldal Wisti, Anne Jørgensen, Susan Möller-Wiering, Camilla Luise Dahl, Kirsten Toftegaard, Anne Batzer, Karin Frei, Morten Ravn, Jette Sidelmann and Sussi Andersen at CTR and Helle Nygaard Bechmann at the Saxo Institute who provided cheer and moral support; CTR Visiting Scholars Brendan Burke and Lorenz Rahmstorf for help with archaeological terms and clarifying the intricacies of German spelling; Søren Rantzau from the Royal Danish Library for advice on library catalogues; Carsten Due-Nielsen at Copenhagen University's Saxo Institute who was willing to share his considerable editing expertise and Sarah Niebe and Mikkel Bach Mortensen who helped with computer glitches; Lone Dalsgaard André at Kolding Design School and her staff, Vibeke Riisberg, Joy Boutrup, Kirsten Nissen and Anne Louise Bang for their useful comments on the manuscript and Annette Grønbæk who took care of the practical arrangements when several of the contributors to this book lectured at Kolding; Lis Thavlov, Rita Lenstrup, Jens Rixen and Bo Søgaard Jensen who all helped with the translation of certain legal expressions; Clare Litt from Oxbow Books who patiently answered elementary questions; and above all to all the contributors to this anthology – the editors' heartfelt praise for a job well done. It has been a privilege to work with you all.

We thank the following for copyright permission: Prof. Christos Doumas, Excavations at Akrotiri, Thera and The Archaeological Society at Athens (Figs 1.1, 1.2); The Lyceum Club of Greek Women Costume Collection (Fig. 1.3); The Archaeological Receipts Fund (T.A.P.A.) and Archaeological Museum of Herakleion (Fig. 1.4); The Museum of Fine Arts, Boston (Fig. 1.5); Getty Images/All Over Press, Photo by Michael Steele (Fig. 1.6); The Trustees of the British Museum (Figs 2.1, 2.2); The Oriental Institute, The University of Chicago (Fig. 2.3); Jona Lendering and Marianne Bloch Hansen (Fig. 2.4); Dr. Sergei Polin, Institute of Archaeology of Ukraine (Figs 2.7–2.9); The Hungarian National Museum, photographer András Dabasi (Figs 3.1, 3.3) and photographer Csaba Barbay

(Figs 3.2, 3.4–3.7); photographer Kit Weiss (Fig. 4.1); photographer Roberto Fortuna, (Figs 4.2–4.5, 4.8); Allan Juhl, Bornholm Museum (Figs 5.1, 5.2); photographer Martin Stoltze, Bornholm Museum (Fig. 5.3); The National Museum of Denmark (Fig. 7.1); Camilla Luise Dahl (Figs 7.2–7.5); photographer Jens Christian Lund (Figs 7.2, 7.3); The Royal Armoury, Stockholm, photographer Göran Schmidt (Figs 8.1, 8.2, 8.4–8.6); National Heritage Board, Stockholm Stockholm Antikvarisk-topografiska arkivet (Fig. 8.3); The National Museum of Denmark, photographer Peter Danstrøm (Figs 9.1–9.3); The National Museum of Denmark, photographer Roberto Fortuna (Figs 9.4, 10.2–10.5, 10.7–10.10, 10.12–10.14, 10.18, 10.20, 10.22); Statens Museum for Kunst (Fig. 9.5); Randers Art Museum, photographer Niels Erik Højerup (Fig. 9.6); photographer Henrik Bjerregrav (Figs. 9.7, 9.9); The Open Air Museum *Den Gamle By*, Århus (Figs 9.8–9.11); Kirsten Toftegaard, Curator of the Textile Collection, Danish Museum of Art and Design (Figs 10. 6, 10.21. Previously published in *Kvinlig mode under två sekel* by B. Hammar and P. Rasmussen, Lund: Signum, 2001); MPTV.NET (Fig. 11.1).

INTRODUCTION

How do we dress the past? What lies behind the dress of a Viking on a mannequin in a museum, the appearance of a Roman emperor in the movie *Gladiator* or an illustration of a Scythian warrior in an archaeological treatise?

Today, there is a growing interest in ancient and historical costume, as well as an increasing need in museums, in the media and in the private sphere to obtain all the available knowledge about the subject. To ensure that this is possible on an adequately scholarly level, the academic community of prehistoric and modern textile research has to put more effort into presenting data and research results in a more user-friendly manner.

The aim of the present volume is to highlight the difficulties in the analysis of archaeological and historical garments and to show how scholars from different disciplines approach the subject. The book is conceived as a handbook by specialists for non-specialists. Our aim is to show the wide range of disciplines involved in textile research, and also the multitude of topics which can be investigated through the study of dress.

The anthology originated in a series of lectures given by The Danish National Research Foundation's Centre for Textile Research to students at the Design School in Kolding, Denmark in spring 2006. The contributors come from a variety of backgrounds such as archaeology, ancient history, ethnology, design, professional weaving, museum and media studies. They have been given a free hand in choosing their perspective and approach to the subject and have selected a number of issues for discussion, in order to demonstrate the importance of being critical of sources when dealing with ancient or historical dress, while presenting their methods, reflections and results.

Our sources when investigating textiles are, first of all, the dresses themselves, both archaeological textiles excavated from the soil, and historical costumes preserved in museum collections. Furthermore, written materials, images, textile tools, context studies of workspaces, industries or household production provide important additional information. Textile researchers also draw data from ethnographical sources and from craftsmanship. Each of these sources informs us in its own way about the prevalent attitude towards the body in different places and periods. Each of them is also problematic in its own way. All of the chapters in this volume demonstrate how important it is to use all available sources critically in order to obtain the most objective picture of dress in the past.

Most authors emphasize the wide range of disciplines studying textiles, dress and costume. It may be significant that none of them sees this as a conflict. On the contrary, there is an awareness of how different disciplines can offer new perspectives and new questions. Today, study of costume is not limited to the basic description. In recent decades, textile research has developed from the object-based, empirical collection of data to a context based approach. We want to know about the use of dress: how did it feel to wear it? For what occasion was it made and/or worn? Was it comfortable? How often was it worn? Why did the wearer choose this garment and textile? We want to know about the context: for what purpose was the textile made or bought? When was it worn? And what impression did the textile give? We want to know about the process of production: how was it organised and who participated in it? Where did the production take place, and why? What tools and what techniques did the producers choose, and what did they base their choice on? We want to know about the costume's history: why was it made and what do the traces of wear tell us? Why has the garment changed in size or function?

Still, it is important to emphasize: the following chapters do not necessarily show how people dressed in the past, rather how we think they dressed in the past, and why we think so.

Traditional research is seen as objective and a search for the *truth*. The papers in this anthology reflect an ongoing process where scholars acknowledge the subjective, intuitive and tactile aspects of knowledge such as feeling, the handle of an object, the know-how or craftsmanship. In textile research, we must supplement the supremacy of the eyes as our primary mode of comprehending the world. We include the tactile sense: corselets and heavy coronation robes immediately give us the sense of tightness and heaviness; rags and worn-out shoes remind us of the harsh cold of a Scandinavian winter.

How do we make the past present? From hobby enthusiasts who devote considerable time and expense to re-enacting the past, to museum curators who spend their entire professional careers recreating the past for the edification of the general public, to historians who recently devoted nearly an entire issue of the journal *History and Theory* to the topic, the past in the present is a burning subject.

Popularising textile knowledge is vital. Textile research is interdisciplinary, and textile scholars are trained to transgress the academic boundaries between conservation and archaeology, history and ethnology. In this publication, we wanted to go a step further: to enter into a dialogue with colleagues in other textile-related fields, such as designers. It is a challenge and, in the process of compiling this book, we have had many discussions about what this new common platform could be. Our experience of teaching at a design school gave hints of a common interest and knowledge, and what we could learn from each other.

We hope that this book will be of equal interest to students of costume design, museology and film, hobby enthusiasts, museum curators, historians and all who are interested in costume – prehistoric, historic or modern – and its impact on human society. This is an invitation to dive into the colourful world of dress.

Margarita Gleba, Cherine Munkholt and Marie-Louise Nosch
Copenhagen, December 2006

In the spirit of collaboration, the Kolding School of Design made a generous gift to this publication: a collage documenting the design process of the clothing projects by the design students in 2006, inspired by our lectures. The collage was made by Kirsten Schou-Jørgensen.

xxii

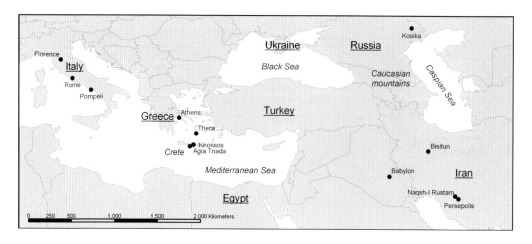

Map 1.

Map 2.

Maps created by Peder Dam

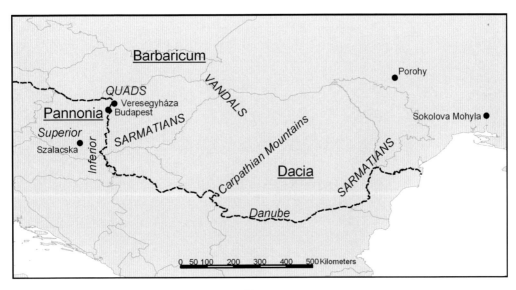

Map 3.

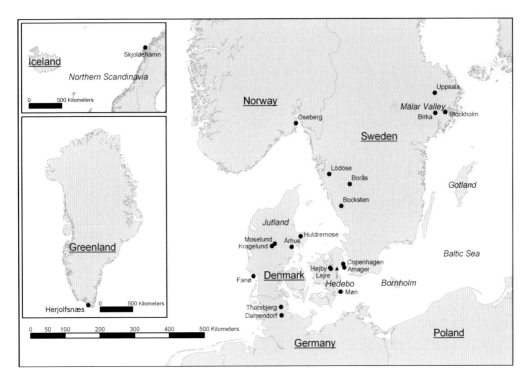

Map 4.

Maps created by Peder Dam

Chapter 1

Haute Couture in the Bronze Age: A History of Minoan Female Costumes from Thera

Marie-Louise B. Nosch

In this chapter, the author presents some of the female costumes from Minoan Santorini and uses recent scholarly contributions as the basis of her discussion on the Bronze Age technology available for the manufacture of these costumes. She views the use and representation of these costumes today as stemming from political and cultural agendas.

Keywords: Minoan, Thera, frescoes, colours, design, historiography.

King Minos was a legendary king at Knossos in Crete. He was married to Queen Pasiphae and had a daughter, Ariadne. According to legend, Minos demanded an annual tribute of seven young men and seven young women from Athens. The young people were sacrificed to his son, the monster Minotaur, half man and half bull, who was kept in a labyrinth. The Athenian prince, Theseus, son of King Aegeus, sailed off on a dangerous mission to Crete: to kill the Minotaur and free Athens from the demand for human tribute. His ship had black sails but he promised his father to raise white sails on his return voyage if his mission was successful. On his arrival in Crete, Ariadne fell in love with Theseus. She gave him a ball of thread to follow through the labyrinth. With this thread, he managed to find his way through the labyrinth, kill the Minotaur, and return safely out of the labyrinth again. Joyful over his success, he immediately travelled back but forgot to change his sails. Aegeus, holding watch for his son's ships from a rock high above the ocean, saw the black sails and out of despair over his son's presumed death, threw himself into the sea.

This classical legend contains two references to textiles: Ariadne's thread and the coloured sails. Let us now follow Ariadne's thread into the world of Minoan textile and costume.

The Minoan culture is named after King Minos. The Minoan civilisation is attested in the Bronze Age in present day Greece and Turkey. One of the centres of Minoan culture was the small island of Thera, today Santorini, in the southern part of the Cycladies in Greece (see Map 1). The island was destroyed in the Bronze Age by a volcanic eruption which blew a major part of the island away.

When did this destruction occur? Specialists agree that it was some time between 1700 and 1500 BC, that is, 3700–3500 years ago. Some scholars, based on the study of ceramic style, date the destruction to 1500 BC; others believe in the dates 1620–1520 or 1700–1610 BC, based on the scientific analyses of changes in the carbon isotopes in finds from the excavation; pieces of wood have been used for dendro-chronology and have yielded the dates 1628–1626 BC; ash layers from the volcanic eruption found in ice-core drillings on Greenland have been dated to 1645 BC. And, recently, analysis of carbon isotopes from a tree trapped in the ash layer has given a destruction date of 1627–1600 (Friedrich *et al.* 2006).

The discussion on the destruction date will probably continue. However, for the purposes of this chapter, it is important to note that the destruction of Thera created a freeze-frame in which Minoan life and material culture was preserved. Thus, the destruction gives us a kind of snap-shot of the life of the last inhabitants.

The island of Thera literally exploded when the volcano erupted. In the remaining part of the island, excavations have been carried out, revealing a Bronze Age town. Similar to Roman Pompeii, the excavators dug into private houses and discovered preserved furniture, cooking ware and amazing frescoes on the walls.

The frescoes show men, women and children in elaborate costumes. Here we will focus on the Minoan frescoes representing women and their costumes. Two excellent examples are the 'Female Figure' (Fig. 1.1) and the 'Saffron gatherers' (Fig. 1.2).

How far is it plausible to believe that the costumes on the Theran frescoes represent real costumes and are not pure fantasy? Elizabeth Barber, the specialist on Aegean textile and costume, believes that the elaborate and "festive" female dresses seen on the monuments were probably a development of daily wear (Barber 1991, 315). In the following discussion, I will outline the technological possibilities in Minoan society for producing such garments.

FEMALE COSTUMES

The female Minoan costume seems to be composed of a tight bodice, sometimes open-fronted and with short sleeves. The bodice is decorated on the edges, either with bands or in-woven decorative motifs. The skirt can be bell-shaped or flounced, and is often decorated with either woven stripes or bands. Figures 1.1 and 1.2 show women and girls wearing sleeved bodices with decorative bands on the shoulders. Tassels hang from the sleeve edges or around the waist. The girls wear what look like wrap-around skirts richly decorated with bands. All the depicted costumes display a wealth of colours and an extended use of bands as decorative elements. Elizabeth Barber writes:

> On the whole, the Theran textiles all look readily – even easily – weavable. To imitate most of these designs, the techniques of choice would be supplemental-warp float for the bands and supplemental weft for the larger cloths, possibly in double-faced or even double-cloth techniques (Barber 1991, 317).

Fig. 1.1: Female figure from the House of the Ladies, Room 1. (The Greek Archaeological Society at Athens, Excavation of Akrotiri, Thera)

Fig 1.2: Saffron gatherers from Xeste 3, Room 3a. (The Greek Archaeological Society at Athens, Excavation of Akrotiri, Thera)

Pictures of Minoan dresses are found on frescoes, seals and statues, and the evidence is scattered all over the Aegean area throughout the 2nd millennium BC. Attempts have been made to see specific developments over time and space, regional differences or ethnic markers. Nevertheless, the relative scarcity of evidence, and the wide time span, makes it difficult to trace such patterns. I would agree with Edith Trnka's assessment of the situation:

Rather than an indicator of ethnicity, differences in design may refer more to the age, status and activity of the wearer. Distinctions like textile patterns, colours and band decorations within the fabrics might indicate the social rank of the wearer (Trnka 2007, 121).

Several attempts have been made through the years to reconstruct the Minoan costumes. In the 1920s, the Lyceum Club of Greek Women made reconstructions of Minoan costumes. The work was done under the guidance of Anna Apostolidou, then Curator of the Museum of Decorative Arts (the present day Museum of Greek Folk Art). The costumes were used for festive events at the Panathenian Stadium in 1927 (Fig. 1.3). About 80 years later, Abby Lillethun made several reconstructions of the bodice of the young saffron gatherer on the Theran fresco and tested how reconstructions fitted the model and matched the frescoes. According to her, the closest match to the images came in the cut-in-one bodice with straight sleeves made of linen, because it fitted closely to the neck of the model; it was comfortable and the fit was smooth and tight (Lillethun 2003). These time-consuming reconstruction tests – among others – are a valuable source when investigating Aegean costume traditions and techniques.

COLOURS AND DYES

The use of colours – blue, yellow and red – springs to the eye when admiring the Minoan female costumes. People of the Bronze Age could obtain variegated shades or patterns with the naturally pigmented black, brown or white wool. However, in the Bronze Age, it is likely that through selective breeding people could increase the production of white wool and this gave great opportunities for an amazing explosion of colours in dress. Textiles were dyed with plant and animal dyes. The colour purple could be obtained from murex mollusc. These are found in the Mediterranean Sea and are edible. When archaeologists find heaps of murex shells, it may thus indicate that the snails were consumed or used to obtain dyestuff. The murex mollusc yields a strong and colourfast dye, varying from red to purple and blue. Extraction of purple from murex was known early in the 2nd millennium BC in Crete (Burke 1999). Murex-dyed garments are also known from later ancient literature: the Roman emperor alone was allowed to wear a purple garment while his senators could only carry purple-dyed bands on their toga. Purple dye from murex has always been considered a costly and luxurious substance, even more so than gold.

In some works on ancient colours and dyes, it is assumed that enormous amounts of murex were required to dye one piece of cloth. This however, is based on a misunderstanding of the dyeing technicalities. In the 19th century AD, the growing chemical industry aimed at supplanting plant and animal dyes with chemical dyes by determining the composition of murex dye and by isolating the pure dye substances. The chemist Paul Friedländer isolated 1.4 g of pure dyestuff from 12,000 *Murex brandaris*, one type of murex molluscs. These calculations have been applied to ancient dyeing technologies, since a precise understanding of the ancient dyeing techniques is lacking.

Fig. 1.3: Costumes in the style of the Mycenaean and Minoan periods. (Courtesy of the Lyceum club of Greek Women Costume Collection).

However, the Minoans did not necessarily need the pure substance for their textiles (Burke 1999). A strong, vivid, and colourfast colour can be obtained with much less murex. This technical misunderstanding, combined with the Theran frescoes and the knowledge of Roman extravagance have contributed to the idea of the Minoan culture as being luxurious and sophisticated.

Roots from the madder plant can also be used for red dyes. We are less sure about the blue colours, but it was probably obtained from woad. The yellow could be obtained from either saffron or safflower flowers. On the Theran frescoes, women gather saffron and we know from the Late Bronze Age inscriptions that safflower was cultivated on palace land, most probably for dye substances to be used in the textile industry (Nosch 2004).

TECHNOLOGY AND THE ORGANISATION OF PRODUCTION

Textiles in Minoan times were made of wool, flax and – possibly – silk (Barber 1991). An intact silk cocoon was found on Thera, and some carved seals depict moths. This may indicate the use of silk already in the Bronze Age. Still, wool was the major fibre in textile production. Analyses of animal bones from excavations of Minoan sites in Crete show that the majority of sheep bones belong to rather old animals. This suggests that sheep were kept for lambing, milk and wool, and only butchered at an old age (Militello 2007). At Thera, archaeo-zoological and palaeo-botanical analyses have shown that wool and flax were available on the island (Tzachili 2007).

Wool or flax fibres were prepared and spun with a drop spindle in the Bronze Age. This process was extremely time-consuming (Andersson and Nosch 2003). When enough thread had been produced, the thread was mounted on a warp-weighted loom. This flexible technology could be used for both plain and pattern weaving.

One would expect to find spindle whorls and loom weights at any Minoan site. Such textile tools are needed to cover even the most basic needs of a Bronze Age community. However, archaeologists encounter an intriguing situation: In Minoan Crete, loom weights are found in abundance, but the finds of spindle whorls are rare (Burke 1997, note 9). In order to weave with the loom weights, the Minoans would have needed to spin – but their spinning tools are missing in the archaeological record. Also at Thera, almost no spindle whorls are attested in the archaeological record (Tzachili 2007). It is even more intriguing that the opposite situation is attested on the sites on mainland Greece: many spindle whorls are found but few loom weights. Scholars are still investigating these peculiar situations. One possibility is that tools of perishable materials were used for spinning in Crete, while the mainlanders used perishable materials – or simply stones – to obtain tension in their warp weighted loom.

The people of Thera probably produced textiles for domestic use as well as for trade: this is suggested by the discovery of a Linear A clay tablet with accounts and the ideogram for textiles. Another fresco at Thera shows ships with sails, and sailcloth must have been important to a population of traders and fishermen.

According to Pietro Militello, textile production in the Minoan Bronze Age shifted and changed nature over the centuries. In the so-called First Palace period, about 2000–1700 BC, textile production was mainly a household activity, but the rising powers of the Minoan palaces required a more specialised production, in particular for gift exchange and creating networks between palaces within the Minoan culture and with foreign powers. In the Second Palace period, about 1700 to 1450 BC, productive centres, the so-called Villas, monitored the textile production, either in the villa itself or outside in the territory under its control. After Thera was destroyed by the eruption, the mainlanders, the Mycenaens, took over Crete. They installed a highly centralised textile production (Militello 2007).

Thera, however, is not a palace site. It is an island town, and thus the theories of palatial structures monitoring textile production cannot be directly applied to the productive activities there. Evidence for weaving is abundant at Thera, and the loom weights show a remarkable uniformity. This may suggest that textile production was, if not controlled, at least coordinated among the town people. The spatial distribution as well may indicate a specialisation of textile production and a concentration in some hands: loom weights are found accumulated in specific town houses. Of the eleven partially or completely excavated houses, only four contain loom weights. In the houses with the ladies in the frescoes (Figs 1.1 and 1.2), no loom weights were found (Tzachili 2007). This suggests that the activities carried out in these houses were not spinning and weaving. Greek archaeologist Iris Tzachili points out that the archaeological evidence from Thera actually conflicts with the traditional idea of ancient textile production being carried out everywhere and by everyone.

Iris Tzachili suggests that textile production at Akrotiri operated in a context involving some kind of women's cooperative, similar to a guild, in which the duties and profits would have been shared, possibly according to the skills of the participants. She makes a stimulating comparison with the fresco of the saffron gatherer (Fig. 1.1): here several women work individually, but collect saffron in similar baskets and deliver the flowers to a collective basket (Tzachili 2007).

INTERPRETING MINOAN DRESS

Nowhere is Minoan costume so well represented as in the frescoes at Thera. However, the elaborate dresses are not a Theran phenomenon: at other Minoan sites such as Hagia Triada and Knossos in Crete, there are fragments of frescoes showing similar costumes. Also, carved seals and figurines show female figures in bodices and skirts. A famous example is the so-called Snake Goddess from Knossos (Fig. 1.4). Her bodice is similar to the other Minoan ladies, but her dress is designed differently and supplemented with an apron.

Naturally, scholars have been questioning the status of the women depicted. Are they ordinary women dressing up for a special occasion? Are they aristocrats? Or are they goddesses? The context in which the women are depicted is exotic and even supernatural.

The items with which they are depicted – saffron and snakes – recall a spiritual and luxurious universe.

During a seminar for a group of design students, I showed a 'Minoan' ivory figurine, now in the Boston Museum of Fine Arts (Fig. 1.5). This figurine has caused many scholarly discussions about its authenticity and the issue is still debated. To my great surprise, the design students who have no scholarly training in art history or archaeology, immediately reacted to the figurine. They found it 'Victorian' and dated it to around AD 1900, based on the design of the dress. In fact, as Kenneth Lapatin has shown, the statuette is probably a fake (Lapatin 2003). It was intriguing how the trained eyes of design students immediately spotted the 19th century style of the figurine's costume. This is to me an example of how design studies can contribute to archaeology and textile research.

Fig 1.4: Knossos Snake Goddess statuette. (The Archaeological Museum of Heraklion)

MINOAN COSTUME IN THE 21ST CENTURY

Can Minoan designs be used in the design process of the 21st century? A pilot study conducted recently in a Greek design school was aimed at merging the Greek past with contemporary design. One of the results was the design of toothbrushes inspired by the Minoan dresses depicted in frescoes from Santorini. Thus, history can sometimes be used as a source of inspiration for innovative design (Perivoliotis 2005).

However, another tendency, that of retrospection or looking back to the past in order to construct a national identity and national design, can also be observed. The Greek design students used Minoan art as 'Hellenic art', and thus established a direct connection between the Bronze Age cultures and today. The aim was to strengthen contemporary Greek design, and in this process, Minoan art contributed to the construction of a modern national identity and of Greek design as a brand. From the historian's point of view, it is interesting how Minoan culture today is integrated in Greek culture, although the Minoans definitely did not speak Greek and the Minoan culture is quite different from the Mycenaean and the later classical Greek cultures. Scholars today emphasise how the Minoan culture is "produced and consumed" by tourists as well as specialists (Hamilakis and Momigliano 2006).

The exotic nature of Minoan culture used to cause perplexity in the (self-) understanding of Greek history. Dancing women with bare breasts were not easy to connect with classical democracy and philosophy. Colourful dresses and veils did not correspond to the traditional picture of Greek white marble statues. In recent years,

Fig 1.5: Statuette of a snake goddess, Museum of Fine Arts, Boston. (Photograph © 2007 Museum of Fine Arts, Boston)

however, the traditional view has been questioned. A powerful manifestation of the integration of the Minoan past into Greek history was the opening ceremony of the Olympic Games in Athens in 2004 (Fig. 1.6). The procession representing Greek history started out with women in Minoan dresses. These colourful costumes thus set a new agenda for both Greek culture and – perhaps – for the fashion industry. Ariadne's thread revealed the secrets of the labyrinth, and Theseus wanted to use his sails as a means of

Fig 1.6: Opening ceremony, Olympic Games, Athens, August 2004. (Photo © Michael Steele/Getty Images/All over Press). See also extracts of opening ceremony on http://www.olympic.org/uk/index_uk.asp>

communication. We are still questioning the message of the Minoan costumes, but without doubt they represent a powerful manifestation of a civilisation communicating its culture through dress.

BIBLIOGRAPHY

On the topic of Bronze Age Mediterranean textiles and dress, the major reference work is by Elizabeth Barber (1991); Comparisons between Minoan, Mycenaean and Homeric textiles and costumes are analyzed in the German monograph, written by the excavator of Thera, Spyridon Marinatos, *Kleidung, Bart- und Haartracht*. Archaeologia Homerica I 1 AB (1967). Methodological difficulties in reconstructing ancient costumes are discussed in a recent paper by Ariane Marcar, Reconstructing Aegean Bronze Age Fashions, in L. Cleland, M. Harlow and L. Llewellyn-Jones (eds) *The Clothed Body in the Ancient World* (2005).

In this chapter, the following works have been used:

Andersson, E. and M.-L. B. Nosch (2003) With a Little Help from my Friends: Investigation of Mycenaean Textiles with the help from Scandinavian Experimental Archaeology. In K.

Polinger Foster and R. Laffineur (eds) *METRON: Measuring the Aegean Age. Proceedings of the 9th International Aegean Conference: New Haven, Yale University, 18–21 April 2002*, Aegaeum 24, 197–205 and table XLV.

Barber, E. J. W. (1991) *Prehistoric Textiles. The Development of Cloth in the Neolithic and Bronze Ages with Special Reference to the Aegean*. Princeton, Princeton University Press.

Burke, B. (1997) The Organization of Textile Production on Bronze Age Crete. In R. Laffineur and P. Betancourt (eds) *TEXHNE. Craftsmen, Craftswomen and Craftsmanship in the Aegean Bronze Age. Proceedings of the 6th international Aegean Conference, Philadelphia, Temple University, April 1996,* Aegaeum 16, 413–422, Table CLX–CLXI.

Burke, B. (1999) Purple and Aegean Textile Trade in the 2nd Millennium B.C. In P. Betancourt, V. Karageorghis, R. Laffineur and W.-D. Niemeier (eds) *Meletemata. Studies in Aegean Archaeology presented to Malcolm H. Wiener as he enters his 65th Year*, Aegaeum 20, 75–82.

Friedrich, W., B. Kromer, M. Friedrich, J. Heinemeier, T. Pfeiffer and S. Talamo (2006) Santorini Eruption Radiocarbon Dated to 1627–1600. *Science* 312, 548.

Hamilakis, Y. and N. Momigliano (eds) (2006) *Archaeology and European Modernity: producing and consuming the 'Minoans',* Creta Antica 7.

Lapatin, K. (2003) *Mysteries of the Snake Goddess. Art, Desire and the Forging of History*. Cambridge, MA: Da Capo Press.

Lillethun, A. (2003) The Reconstruction of Aegean Cloth and Clothing. In K. Polinger Foster and R. Laffineur (eds) *METRON: Measuring the Aegean Age. Proceedings of the 9th International Aegean Conference: New Haven, Yale University, 18–21 April 2002*, Aegaeum 24, 463–472, plates XCV–XCVII.

Militello, P. (2007) Textile industry and Minoan Palaces. In C. Gillis and M.-L. B. Nosch (eds) *Ancient Textiles. Production, Craft and Society,* Ancient Textiles Series 1, Oxford, Oxbow Books, 35–43.

Nosch, M.-L. B. (2004) Red Coloured Textiles in the Linear B Inscriptions. In L. Cleland and K. Staers (eds) *Colour in the Ancient Mediterranean World*. BAR International Series 1267, 32–39.

Papantoniou, I. and M. Passe-Kotsou (1991) Costumes in the style of the Mycenaean and Minoan periods (Lyceum Club of Greek Women Costume Collection). Commentary. *Diary 1991,* Lyceum Club of Greek Women, 2.

Perivoliotis, M. C. (2005) The Role of Textile History in Design Innovation: A Case Study Using Hellenic Textile History. *Textile History 36, 1–19.*

Trnka, E. (2007), Similarities and Distinctions of Minoan and Mycenaean Textiles. In C. Gillis and M.-L. B. Nosch (eds) *Ancient Textiles. Production, Craft and Society,* Ancient Textiles Series 1, Oxford, Oxbow Books, 120–122.

Tzachili, I. (2007) Weaving at Akrotiri, Thera: defining cloth-making activities as a social process in a Late Bronze Age Aegean town. In C. Gillis and M.-L. B. Nosch (eds) *Ancient Textiles. Production, Craft and Society,* Ancient Textiles Series 1, Oxford, Oxbow Books, 190–196.

Chapter 2

You Are What You Wear: Scythian Costume as Identity

Margarita Gleba

Costume has been regarded as one of the main identifying criteria for Scythians, nomadic peoples who inhabited the Eurasian steppes in the 1st millennium BC. The sources for our understanding of Scythian clothing include ancient literary references, iconographic material and archaeological remains. Each of these sources is imbued with inherent or interpretational problems, which we have to take into account when using them to reconstruct Scythian costume. By combining a variety of sources, the bias of each taken separately is reduced, thereby giving us more insight into what Scythians wore.

Keywords: Scythian, identity, iconography, Greek, Persian, archaeology.

Dress reflects the identity of an individual or a group of peoples more than most other aspects of material culture since it combines both technological achievements and aesthetic values of society. In a way, clothes are a language in which individual garments constitute vocabulary. The study of the costume of ancient societies not only helps in reconstructing the appearance of various peoples, but also opens up numerous aspects of their history: knowing the vocabulary helps to understand the language. Such study is, however, not an easy task as very little direct evidence of clothing has survived in the archaeological record for most ancient cultures. Ancient dress is a foreign language in which, in addition, a lot of words are missing. Textiles and other materials from which garments were made are seldom preserved. Even when they survive, the corpus of finds is in itself biased since the vast majority of ancient clothing is found in burials, usually wealthy burials. The reconstruction of ancient clothing thus has to rely heavily on literary, iconographic and archaeological sources.

Costume has been regarded as one of the main iconographic identifying criteria for Scythians, a collective name given to a group of nomadic peoples of Central-Asian origin, who occupied the steppe regions of Eurasia (modern day Ukraine and Russia) from the 7th through the 3rd century BC (see Map 2). Already in the 5th century BC, the Greek historian Herodotus describes the costume of one of the Scythian tribes in his catalogue of the Persian king Xerxes' troops:

> The Sacae, who are Scythians, had on their tall caps, erect and stiff and tapering to a point; they wore breeches, and carried their native bows, and daggers, and axes withal, which they call "sagaris". These were Amyrgian Scythians, but were called Sacae; for that is the Persian name for all the Scythians (Herodotus 7.64 Loeb translation).

The important detail in this description is the tall pointed hat, which Herodotus calls *kyrbasia*. At another point in his narrative, he mentions that headgear, belts and girdles of Scythians were decorated with gold (Herodotus 1.215).

Another written source of information about Scythians is contained in roughly contemporary Achaemenid Persian inscriptions, which mention three groups of Scythians or Sakai. One of these groups is specified as pointed-hat Scythians. The name indicates that for the Persians, too, clothing in general and the hat in particular has served as an ethnic indicator.

Thus, in both Greek and Persian written sources, Scythians are identified by and with their clothing. Scythians themselves left no written sources, so for historical information we are left to rely on Greek and Achaemenid Persian accounts, which are few and not always reliable. The information in the texts, however, is very scant and often too general, so that for any further investigation of Scythian clothing we must rely on other sources.

What tangible evidence do we have today that would help us reconstruct the way Scythians looked, and how reliable is it? In the following pages the available evidence is examined with a critical eye on the sources. In particular, I will consider the relevant iconography and archaeological finds, supplementing them with and contrasting them to literary sources as a method of arriving at a more comprehensive understanding of Scythian costume in particular, and ancient dress in general.

SCYTHIAN COSTUME IN GREEK ICONOGRAPHY

Greek vase-painting constitutes one of the most frequently used sources for the study of ancient clothing. Until quite recently, Western scholarship has focused on Attic vase-painting as a primary archaeological source of information on the appearance of foreigners. Dress in particular, along with weaponry and, less frequently, phenotype has been used as a criterion for identification of Scythians and other barbarian peoples known from contemporary literature (Raeck 1981, 2).

Most of the representations of what have been identified as Scythian archers on Attic vases belong to the years between 530 and 500 BC (Vos 1963). Their typical attire includes the tall pointed cap with flaps on the sides and back, and the dress consisting of a long-sleeved top and jacket with trousers, all made of patterned material and trimmed with decorated strips along the seams (Figs 2.1–2.2). Few of the archers, however, wear precisely this costume. Scholars explain some variants as being simplifications or elaborations of a decorative sort. The telling implements are often reduced to weapons and the tall pointed cap. Thus, in many cases, Scythian attire has not been used in a specific ethnic sense, but rather employed either to represent a wider range of Asians, or to indicate the function of archer and/or his mythical character (Pinney 1983, 130, 137). Note that the evidence discussed here is exclusively for the male costume.

Scythian clothing as a symbol of archery has been suggested as an explanation for its adaptation for the images of Amazons in Greek art (Bothmer 1957; Vos 1963, *passim*). It can also be associated with their presumed geographical origin in the Black Sea region. Starting about 550 BC, Amazons are depicted with iconographic features of foreign races, such as Persians and Scythians. The most frequent Scythian elements on Amazons include the pointed cap, bow, and *gorytus* or arrow holder. Often Thracian, Scythian, Oriental and Greek elements are intermixed. Thus Amazons are often depicted wearing what are believed to be Scythian garments, yet fighting with Thracian weapons; the combination was possibly intended to emphasize their exotic and mythical aspect (Shapiro 1983, 111).

Fig. 2.1: Scythian archer, Greek black-figure vase, the British Museum. (© British Museum, The Trustees of the British Museum)

It appears, thus, that ethnic identity based on garments can become blurred in cases where Amazons are depicted in Scythian dress or in scenes where the Scythian archers fight on both conflicting sides (Pinney 1983, 131). The simple explanation that people depicted wearing foreign clothing are foreigners, is not valid in every case. Dress and weapons as ethnic indicators are thus flexible within Greek iconography. A paradoxical development of this flexibility appears on the group of so-called Negro alabastra (Neils 1980). These vessels date to the first quarter of the 5th century BC and depict Amazons or, more frequently, Africans wearing a version of the Scythian costume: patterned

Fig. 2.2: Scythian archer, Greek red-figure vase, the British Museum. (© British Museum, The Trustees of the British Museum)

trousers, jacket, often covered by a corselet, usually without pointed hat, but with *gorytus*.

   To what extent does Athenian vase painting reflect the appearance of Scythians then? Ancient literature suggests that Greeks could differentiate between various groups of foreigners, and did so partially on the basis of their clothing. However, it is difficult to know if the people shown on vases wearing garments corresponding to descriptions in texts are, in fact, Scythians or other foreigners. Most arguments rest on the iconography alone. Some scholars generally do not seem to question the results of such identifications (Schauenburg 1975, 106). The iconography itself is, however, often inconsistent and many figures cannot be precisely categorized as 'Scythians' (Miller 1991, 61). After the 5th century BC, Amazons, Persians and generic Easterners in vase painting usually wear eastern garments not necessarily particular to their origin. Descriptions by Herodotus are often used as a confirmation of their identity, yet his accounts, as mentioned above, are short and very general and should be used with caution in modern interpretations of iconography.

We also have to take into account the fact that artistic conventions played a major role in vase-painting in general and in the representation of foreigners in particular (Raeck 1981, 2–3). The appearance of barbarians on vases is based not only on historical reality, but also on artistic canons and it is difficult, if not impossible, to differentiate between the two (Raeck 1981, 3; Miller 1991, 63).

The source of the craftsmen's familiarity with Scythian appearance is yet another problem for us. For many years, the appearance of Scythian archers in Attic painting has been explained by their unsubstantiated presence in Athens between 540 and 500 BC. This premise still underlines Vos' monograph on Scythian archers (Vos 1963, 61–80). Yet, Scythian archers disappear from the vases at the time when Scythians are known to have been brought to Athens (Pinney 1983, 131).

Thus, although Greek vase-painting offers some understanding of the appearance of foreigners, we have to treat it with caution as a class of evidence. Furthermore, the question of whether vase-painting reflects everyday life or represents mythological scenes is still unresolved. The problems in distinguishing different foreigners in Attic vase-painting – if one assumes that the depictions are indeed of foreigners – show the limitations of the material for the understanding of Scythian costume. Although representations on vases are frequently used as documents of the time in which they were painted, the approach is sound only when the information gained from them can be checked against external evidence. In fact, there is quite a diverse body of iconographic and archaeological evidence for Scythian clothing of non-Greek origin.

SCYTHIAN COSTUME IN PERSIAN ICONOGRAPHY

The bas-reliefs of the Apadana in Persepolis (modern Iran), the great Achaemenid centre built in the reign of the most famous of Persian kings, Darius (522–486 BC), represent one such contemporary source of information (Schmidt 1953). The reliefs originally showed the enthroned king in the centre, while processions of gift-bearers of various nations, whose costumes were carefully rendered by the artists, moved towards him. The qualifier 'pointed-hat' found in Achaemenid written sources has led to the plausible identification of one group of gift-bearers as Scythians (Fig. 2.3).

On another monument, the elaborately carved façade of the Tomb of Darius at Naqsh-i-Rustam, the Persian king is represented on a throne supported by various peoples representing different parts of the Persian Empire. Here, three types of Scythians are shown and labelled, which is important considering that there is not much difference in their appearance except in the shape of their hats. Finally, the rock relief at Bisitun, carved in 520–519 BC, during the reign of King Darius, to commemorate his victories over the rebel kings, shows them roped together at the neck. The last one is a Saka prisoner labelled as such (Fig. 2.4); but he also stands out by his very tall hat. Other Persian representations of Scythians occur on cylinder seals showing battles between Persians and Scythians or Scythians by themselves (Minns 1913, 61).

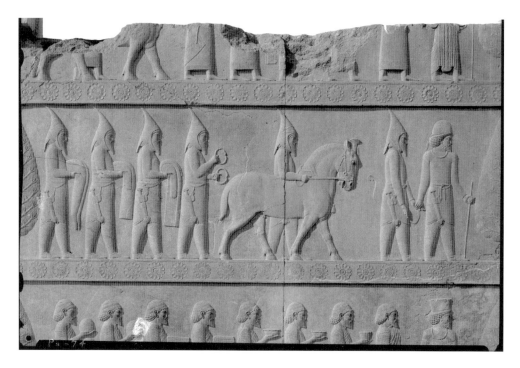

Fig. 2.3: Scythian delegation, Apadana reliefs, Persepolis, Iran. (Courtesy of the Oriental Institute of the University of Chicago)

Persian depictions appear to be more precise renditions of Scythians than Greek vase paintings. However, it is difficult to identify exactly to which of the three earlier mentioned groups the Scythians in Persian reliefs belong to, as hat types and other articles of clothing do not fall precisely into three mutually exclusive groups recorded in the inscriptions (Miller 1991, 62). Artistic conventions hamper our understanding of the details of the costume. And, once again, the evidence is only for male costume.

SCYTHIAN ICONOGRAPHY

Besides Greek and Persian iconography of Scythians, the largest and most important body of evidence for the study of Scythian costume comes, not surprisingly, from Scythia itself. This material includes stone sculpture, toreutic arts or metalwork, clothing appliqués, actual textiles and implements used for the production of clothing (Artamonov 1969; Rolle *et al.* 1991; Rolle 1989; Reeder 1999; Aruz *et al.* 2000). These Scythian sources provide us with important information about not only male, but also for the first time, female Scythian clothing.

Based on the apparent lack of human imagery in early metal work, it has long been assumed, that the Scythians had no significant tradition of anthropomorphic representation. Scythian art has often been categorized as 'nomadic' or 'animal' art. This view, however, is contradicted by a Scythian tradition of monumental stone anthropomorphic images.

Scythian stone statues have not been sufficiently written about in English and are not well known to Western scholars. These unquestionably Scythian monuments, however, have been used as important indicators of the geographical spread of Scythian culture in the Black Sea area. They have been found in the wide geographic area from Romanian Dobrudja in the west to the northern Caucasian mountains in the east, and mark the territory of Scythian dominion in the northern Black Sea region (Bilozor 1991, 161). Over 140 statues dated to the 7th through the 4th centuries BC are known. Predominantly images of warriors, they marked the burial mounds or *kurhany* of especially wealthy individuals (Olchovsky and Evdokimov 1994; Olchovsky 2005). Various interpretations of these stone warriors suggest that they may be portraits of either heroized, deceased chieftains, depictions of ancestral figures, or images of war gods (Popova 1976, 120–121; Olchovsky 2005, 114–117). Whatever their significance, these statues are believed to have been carved by Scythian craftsmen, and are likely to reflect the appearance of real warriors.

The most typical attributes of sculptures representing warriors are various weapons, which, in the best examples, reflect real objects found in burials (Fig. 2.5). Most stone warriors wear jackets

Fig. 2.4: Rock relief at Bisitun, Iran, detail of the Saka prisoner. (Drawing by Marianne Bloch Hansen after photo by Jona Lendering)

or kaftans. Some examples have rich protective armour. Relatively frequent in the archaic statues are helmets and hats, sometimes with a carved pointed end hanging in the back (as in Fig. 2.5). The vast majority of statues have belts, often represented as if made of metal plates. Torques or neck rings represent another ubiquitous attribute. Occasionally, earrings and bracelets are depicted. All of these elements, including parts of armour, have also been found in Scythian graves.

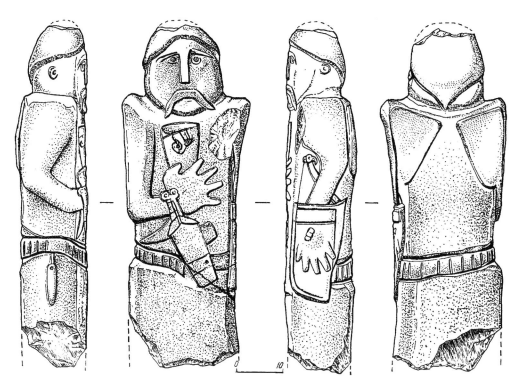

Fig. 2.5: Scythian stone stele from Ternivka, Ukraine. (After Olchovsky and Evdokimov 1994, Fig. 8)

As mentioned earlier, the vast majority of the Scythian stone statues depict males. There is however, a female statue from Pregradnaya, in Russia (Fig. 2.6). This is a unique and unusual example. Because of its singularity, monumental size, original location and the fact that it stood together with two other, male statues, it is believed to have been a cult statue, possibly representing a deity. She wears a long, heavily pleated dress tied with a belt around her waist. A heavy cloak hangs from her shoulders. Her head is covered with a shoulder-length veil. She is shown wearing earrings and an elaborate torque (Olchovsky and Evdokimov 1994, 34).

Scythian stone sculpture does pose some interpretive problems since it was made apparently for a specific purpose, with certain details emphasized and others underplayed. Nevertheless, this body of material is extremely important in the corpus of Scythian material culture and should be studied together with other evidence since it reflects a Scythian view of themselves closer than any other source.

Scythians in their complete attire also appear in the toreutic art of the northern Black Sea area. Gold and silver objects from Ukrainian and Russian burial mounds Kul Oba, Voronezhskiy, Chortomlyk, Haimanova Mohyla and Solokha bear representations of Scythian men with astonishing details of their appearance, including hair, clothing, shoes and weapons, giving a visual expression to Herodotus' description of Sacae.

Scythian jackets are clearly tailored and fur-trimmed along the edges (Fig. 2.7). According to Barber (1994, 133), ancient tunics developed in two major ways. The simpler variety consisted merely of a big rectangular cloth draped over the body and pinned, tied or belted in place. Such garments were typical for ancient Greece. The more complicated type of tunic consisted of several pieces of cloth sewn together to create a sleeved garment. This was the type used by Scythians. With such garments there was no need for pins or fibulae and, in fact, very few fibulae have been found in Scythian burials.

The tailoring is frequently empha-sized in representations of Scythian garments. This purposeful decoration also permits us to reconstruct the way Scythian garments were tailored with some certainty. A gold-plaited silver bowl from Haymanova Mohyla (Fig. 2.8), dated to the 4th century BC, depicts Scythians in such splendidly fashioned dress. The long jackets or kaftans are most likely of embroidered, fur-trimmed leather. An element particular to the Black Sea representations of Scythian clothing is the addition, all round the bottom of such jackets, of long pointed flaps, which must have waved up and down very effectively during horse riding (Rolle 1989, 58; Klochko 1991, 105).

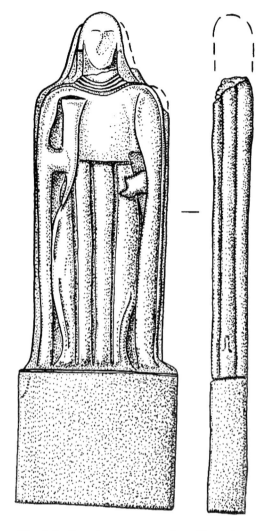

Fig. 2.6: Female stone statue from Pregradnaya, Russia. (After Olchovsky and Evdokimov 1994, Fig. 74)

Trousers in iconography are of both narrow and wide types. These are always elaborately decorated. Besides the tell-tale Scythian appliqués, patterned textiles were most likely used for this purpose. As mentioned before, the decorative elements on garments have been placed in such a manner as to highlight the edges and the seams. Seams especially were emphasized with embroidery. In Slavic folk costumes even today

Fig. 2.7: Scythian gold helmet from Peredriyiva Mohyla, Ukraine. (Courtesy of Dr. Sergei Polin, Institute of Archaeology of Ukraine)

embroidery is generally located at the seams and the openings of the clothing, such as neck-hole, wrists and shirttail. This decoration supposedly was meant to discourage demons from crawling in at the openings (Barber 1994, 163). Whatever the purpose of such specific decorating of dress in Scythian toreutics, its detailed depiction indicates intimate knowledge of the nature of Scythian dress on the part of the artists who made these objects.

The pointed cap, the main iconographic indicator of Scythians in Greek vase-painting, is not a frequent attribute on metalware from Scythian burials. Only vases from Kul Oba and Voronezskiy bear depictions of Scythians wearing such headgear and these caps are not nearly as tall and elaborate as those in Greek representations. The rest of the Black Sea material shows Scythians bare-headed.

Also depicted on metal vessels is a special type of Scythian boots. They were tied to the feet with narrow laces under the ankle or around the foot itself, as depicted on the bowl from Haymanova Mohyla. Incidentally, such shoes are not depicted in Greek vase-painting.

Fig. 2.8: Scythian figures on a bowl from Haymanova Mohyla, Ukraine. (Courtesy of Dr. Sergei Polin, Institute of Archaeology of Ukraine)

FEMALE SCYTHIAN COSTUME

Considerably less is known about the dress of Scythian women than about male garments. Ancient literature does not provide us with any descriptions and there are no known representations of Scythian women's clothing in Greek vase-painting or Persian art. All information comes from the Black Sea material, and although there are significantly fewer depictions of women than men, and these images most likely reflect the appearance of the elite members of the society, these depictions do give some understanding of their appearance. Apart from the single female stone statue discussed earlier, clothing plaques and headdress parts constitute the only other class of representational material.

The nearly identical plaques depicting a seated female figure wearing a long dress, a headdress and a cloak covering the headdress and falling down behind her shoulders, with a man standing in front of her, have been found in several Scythian burial mounds (Fig. 2.9). Another example is a 4th-century BC gold cone-shaped plaque from a headdress found in Karagodeuashkh, in Russia. Here, the scene is divided into three registers, the lowest of which depicts a frontally seated woman flanked by two female and two male attendants. She wears a long pleated dress and a tall headdress with a veil or cloak with decorated edges hanging down from it behind her back. Behind the seated woman stand two other women, wearing hood-like head covers. One more representation of a female appears on a diadem from Sakhnivka in Ukraine. On this object, again, a woman wears a long robe and a tall headdress.

Most scholars agree that the females depicted in all these plaques are goddesses (Jacobson 1995, 164–165). Nevertheless, their garments are representative of what real Scythian women may have worn. Thus the women of the upper social levels probably wore long dresses, and over these long richly ornamented coats. On their heads they wore magnificent headdresses of various forms frequently covered with veils.

The style and representation within the metal work of the Scythians is problematic to some extent since it is impossible to deny that the handling of human figures on

Fig. 2.9: Scythian gold plaque with seated goddess from Chortomlyk, Ukraine. (Courtesy of Dr. Sergei Polin, Institute of Archaeology of Ukraine)

many objects derives from Hellenic taste (Jacobson 1995, 72). The apparent lack of anthropomorphic images mentioned earlier has led to the assumption that the best gold work from Scythia, and especially those objects adorned with human representations, has been manufactured by Greek craftsmen, ostensibly making them less 'reliable' in terms of what they can tell us about Scythian appearance. Yet, even if Greek craftsmen could have conceived and executed these human figures, it would still be impossible to find convincing models for these representations within surviving Greek art. Whatever the nationality or ethnicity of the craftsmen, the details of clothing in representations discussed above undeniably point to their close familiarity with Scythian people.

ARCHAEOLOGICAL EVIDENCE

Finally, a crucial source in our quest to reconstruct Scythian costume is archaeological material. As in the case of other sources, it is not without problems, the most significant of which is the fragmentariness of remains, making the identification of specific garments and their function very difficult. Here, too, we can get a glimpse of only the wealthiest levels of society. The latter factor makes the possibility of imports among materials and even clothes themselves quite likely, so it is hard to judge how typical the surviving fragments are for the overall picture of Scythian garments. Nonetheless, some information about Scythian dress can be gleaned from these scanty remains.

Gold appliqués

As mentioned in the beginning, Herodotus informs us that a characteristic element of Scythian clothing was the application of golden plaques on the clothing. In fact, such plaques are often found in wealthy burials of the Scythian aristocracy. The ornamentation of clothing with appliqués is also attested by representations on Scythian objects and even in Attic vase-painting.

In Western scholarly literature, clothing plaques have been studied mostly from the iconographic standpoint (Jacobson 1995). When found *in situ*, however, they are also extremely useful for partial reconstruction of the original dress. We can frequently trace the contours of the garments through the location of ornaments. The exact position of plaques *in situ* in this case is crucial for our understanding of the appearance of the garment. Thus, dresses have been reconstructed for men and women buried in the Ukraninan *kurhany* of Piski, Kazenna Mohyla, Tovsta Mohyla, Zolota Mohyla (Klochko 1979; 1991). Women's shoes, in fact, could only be reconstructed from the position of golden ornaments in burials, as, for example, in Tovsta Mohyla and Melitopol, also in Ukraine.

A great deal of work has been done on reconstructing women's headdresses. The majority of the gold ornaments found in female burials are, in fact, parts of the elaborate hats of various shapes. They range from simple diadems to close-fitting caps, to magnificent affairs over 30 cm high, sometimes called *kalathoi*. Various head decorations have been reconstructed with varied degree of accuracy from the material found in Chortomlyk, Kamyanka, Berdiansk and Tovsta Mohyla (Klochko 1991, 107–109; Rolle 1989, 60; Rolle, Murzin and Alekseev 1998, 144–45, pl. 24, colour pls 15–18). They bring to life headdresses depicted in the representational art discussed before.

Textiles

In some cases, leather, felt and textiles of various types have survived in burials. Often traces of colour and few remains of thread indicate that the original clothing was colourful, a piece of information which cannot be gained from the representational arts. Textile and leather remains are also our only reliable evidence for the materials and techniques used to make the garments.

From the 4th–3rd century BC *kurhan* Velyka Ryzhanivka in Ukraine, six different textiles have been recovered, consisting of wool, plant (hemp, ramie), and mixed fibres (Babenko, Bredis and Klocho 2001; Bredis 2001). As far as techniques go, there are fragments woven in plain weave and in twill, but one of the pieces is embroidered and another possibly shows evidence of tapestry weave. Numerous fragments of fabric have been recovered at Chortomlyk (Rolle, Murzin and Alekseev 1998, 22–24). Nine woollen pieces have preserved their original red and green colours. Some leather and felt fragments have been found as well. Semibratniy Kurgan 4, in South Russia, dated to the 5th century BC, yielded an interesting piece of resist-painted woollen cloth (Barber 1991, 206–209). A sarcophagus cover from the later Kurgan 6 at the same site was also resist-painted; the same burial yielded pieces of delicate tapestry that must have formed part of the funeral clothing

(Stephani 1881, 119–124). Finally, Pavlovskiy Kurgan, in Ukraine dated to the 4th century BC had preserved pieces of embroidered cloth among the bones of a woman in a sarcophagus. Both resist-painting and embroidery are techniques considered to have originated in the East. Scythians may have transmitted these techniques for the Greeks. The Semibratniy burials also yielded some silk of Chinese origin, and it is likely that Scythians played an important role in the early silk trade. In connection to this, another body of archaeological material has to be considered.

Unique finds come from the Altai Mountains in Siberia. Here, complete costumes were preserved frozen on the bodies in burials (Rudenko 1970; Polosmak and Barkova 2005). The first glimpse of these costumes came in the 1940s with excavations of five burial mounds at Pazyryk. These finds are now in the Hermitage Museum in St. Petersburg. More recent excavations at Ak-Alakha and other Ukok sites have added substantially to our knowledge and understanding of the Pazyryk costumes. All of this material dates to the 5th–3rd centuries BC. Although representing a more eastern and broader Scytho-Siberian culture, these finds should be considered in the study of Scythian dress, especially since many of them constitute complete articles of clothing. Thus, in Kurgan 2 of Pazyryk, an almost intact man's hemp shirt was found. It was sewn from four panels between which sleeves were inserted, with seams emphasized with red woollen thread. It closely resembles Scythian shirts represented on the metalware discussed earlier. Kurgan 2 also produced a female upper garment of squirrel skin, breeches, part of a kaftan with applied leather cut-out decoration with gold disks, similar to the clothing plaques found in the Black Sea area.

Textile tools

Within any society, the physical appearance of dress is limited by aesthetic standards of the culture which in turn are limited by technology. That is why technological evidence for textile production has to be considered here as well. Andersson in this anthology has aptly demonstrated that technical aspects of clothing can be investigated through implements used for its production.

In Scythia, this information is scarce, mostly because of the lack of interest on the part of excavators. However, some examples provided here suggest yet another route for our study of Scythian clothing. Spinning is documented by a few, occasionally preserved spindles that have been found in burials. For example, a beautifully made silver spindle was found in Chortomlyk (Rolle, Murzin and Alekseev 1998, 22 no. 119, pl. 36.2). Numerous spindle whorls of various types also survive. The settlement of Bilske Horodyshche, in Ukraine, dated to the 7th–3rd centuries BC, produced over 400 whorls of 17 types (Jakovenko 1991, 112). It is unclear, what kind of loom Scythians utilized. Barber (1991) believes that inhabitants of the geographic areas north of the Mediterranean utilized the warp-weighted loom, which is unique in that it is archaeologically traceable through the presence of ceramic loom weights. On the territory of Scythia, however, loom weights are rare and, when found, are associated with Greek settlements, thus we may have to look at other possibilities. Still, technical aspects of recovered textiles and the presence of spinning and weaving equipment within the archaeological assemblage of Scythia indicate that at least some parts of the garments were manufactured locally.

CONCLUSIONS

Reconstructing dress and, through it, peoples' identity is not an easy task. We have to consider all the material carefully, taking into account its various limitations, since all evidence is biased and unreliable in some way. Thus, Greek, Persian and Scythian depictions emphasize different aspects of the appearance of Scythians. That is why we need to study all the material to learn about their clothing. By combining literary, iconographic and archaeological evidence, the bias of each taken separately is significantly reduced. All this material allows us to draw some general conclusions about Scythian appearance and learn more about their identity as perceived by other ancient peoples. To what extent we are able to understand the language of dress depends greatly on how carefully we study the vocabulary.

ACKNOWLEDGEMENT

I would like to thank Sergei Polin for reading and making valuable comments to the first draft of this chapter and for his help with illustrations; Marianne Bloch Hansen kindly provided a new drawing for Fig. 2.4. I also thank Sergey Yatsenko, whose important book on the costume of Indo-Iranian peoples (Yatsenko 2006) appeared since this article went to press.

BIBLIOGRAPHY

Artamonov, M. I. (1969) *The Splendor of Scythian Art*. New York, Frederick A. Prager.

Aruz, J. *et al.* (2000) *The Golden Deer of Eurasia. Scythian and Sarmatian Treasures from the Russian Steppes*. New York, The Metropolitan Museum of Art.

Babenko, T. N., N. Y. Bredis and L. S. Klochko (2001) Фрагменты ткани из мужского захоронения в Большом Рыжановском кургане. *Восточноевропейский археологический журнал* 2 (9).

Barber, E. J. W. (1991) *Prehistoric Textiles. The Development of Cloth in the Neolithic and Bronze Ages*. Princeton, Princeton University Press.

Barber, E. W. (1994) *Women's Work: The First 20,000 Years. Women, Cloth, and Society in Early Times*. Princeton, Princeton University Press.

Bilozor, V. P. (1991) Skythische Grossplastik aus Stein. In R. Rolle *et al.* (eds) *Gold der Steppe Archäologie der Ukraine*. Schleswig, Archäologisches Landesmuseum, 161–164.

Bothmer, D. von (1957) *Amazons in Greek Art*. Oxford, Clarendon Press.

Bredis, N. Y. (2001) Исследование скифского текстиля (нач. III в. до н.э.) из Большого Рыжановского кургана. *Восточноевропейский археологический журнал 4 (11)*.

Jacobson, E. (1995) *The Art of the Scythians: The Interpretation of Cultures at the Edge of the Hellenic World*. New York, E. J. Brill.

Jakovenko, E. V. (1991) Skythische Spindeln. In R. Rolle *et al.*, (eds) *Gold der Steppe. Archäologie der Ukraine*. Schleswig, Archäologisches Landesmuseum, 111–113.

Klochko, L. S. (1979) Реконструкція скіфськіх головних жіночіх уборів (за матер'ялами Червоноперекопськіх курганів). *Arkheologiya* 31, 16–28.

Klochko, L. S. (1991) Skythische Tracht. In Rolle, *et al.* (eds) *Gold der Steppe Archäologie der Ukraine*. Schleswig, Archäologisches Landesmuseum, 105–111.

Miller, M. (1991) Foreigners at the Greek Symposium? In W. J. Slater (ed.) *Dining in a Classical Context*. Ann Arbor, University of Michigan Press.

Minns, E. H. (1913) *Scythians and Greeks: A Survey of Ancient History and Archaeology on the North Coast of the Euxine from the Danube to the Caucasus*. Cambridge, Cambridge University Press.

Neils, J. (1980) The Group of the Negro Alabastra: A Study in Motif Transferal. *Antike Kunst* 23, 13–23.

Olchovsky, V. S. (2005) *Монументальная скульптура населения западной части евразийских степей эпохи раннего железа*. Moscow, Nauka.

Olchovsky, V. S. and G. L. Evdokimov (1994) *Скифские изваяния VII–III вв. до н. э.* Moskow: RAN (Russian Academy of Sciences) and UAN (Ukrainian Academy of Sciences).

Pinney, G. F. (1983) Achilles Lord of Scythia. In W. G. Moon (ed.) *Ancient Greek Art and Iconography*. Madison, The University of Wisconsin Press, 127–146.

Polosmak, N. V. and L. L. Barkova (2005) Костюм и текстиль пазырыкцев Алтая (IV–III вв. до н. э.) Novosibirsk, Infolio.

Popova, E. A. (1976) Об истоках традиций и эволюции форм скифской скульптуры. *Sovetskaja Archeologija* 1, 108–122.

Raeck, W. (1981) *Zum Barbarenbild in der Kunst Athens im 6. und 5. Jahrhundert v. Chr.* Bonn, Rudolf Habelt.

Reeder, E. (ed.) (1999) *Scythian Gold. Treasures from Ancient Ukraine*. New York, Harry N. Abrams.

Rolle, R. (1989) *The World of Scythians*. Berkeley, University of California Press.

Rolle, R. *et al.* (eds) (1991) *Gold der Steppe. Archäologie der Ukraine*. Schleswig: Archäologisches Landesmuseum.

Rolle, R., Murzin, V. J. and A. J. Alekseev (1998) *Königskurgan Certomlyk: ein skythischer Grabhügel des 4. vorchristlichen Jahrhunderts*. Mainz, Verlag Phillip von Zabbern.

Rudenko, S. I. (1970) *Frozen Tombs of Siberia: the Pazyryk Burials of Iron Age Horsemen*. Berkeley, University of California Press.

Schauenburg, K. (1975) ΕΥΡΥΜΕΔΩΝ ΕΙΜΙ. *Athenische Mitteilungen* 90, 97–121.

Schmidt, E. F. (1953) *Persepolis I*. Chicago, University of Chicago Press.

Shapiro, H. A. (1983) Amazons, Thracians, and Scythians. *Greek Roman and Byzantine Studies* 24, 105–115.

Stephani, L. (1881) *Compte-Rendu de la Commission Impériale Archéologique (1878–1879)*, St. Petersburg.

Vos, M. F. (1963) *Scythian Archers in Archaic Attic Vase-Painting*. Groningen, J. B. Wolters.

Yatsenko, S. A. (2006) Костюм Древней Евразии. Moskow, Vostochnaya Literatura.

Chapter 3

"On the Borders of East and West": A Reconstruction of Roman Provincial and Barbarian Dress in the Hungarian National Museum

Ilona Hendzsel, Eszter Istvánovits, Valéria Kulcsár, Dorottya Ligeti, Andrea Óvári and Judit Pásztókai-Szeőke

The authors of this chapter describe how they reconstructed the clothing of a Roman merchant and four Barbarians living outside the Roman province of Pannonia around the 2nd to the 3rd centuries AD. The reconstructions were created for the new permanent archaeological exhibition "On the Borders of East and West", which opened in November 2002 at the Hungarian National Museum in Budapest. The chapter focuses on the visual representation and methods of reconstruction of the garments of different tribes living in the Carpathian Basin during the Roman Age.

Keywords: Pannonia, Roman, Barbarian, ethnicity, foot-wear, accessories, embroidery, Germanic, Sarmatian.

The visitor entering the Hungarian National Museum's hall presenting Roman Iron Age finds encounters a market scene. The interior arrangement of the room reflects the cultural and geographical division of the Carpathian Basin in Roman times: the Roman province *Pannonia* is exhibited on the visitor's left, while the right side of the hall displays the so-called *Barbaricum*, a territory that was outside and independent of the Roman Empire (Istvánovits and Kulcsár 2005; Rezi Kató and Vasáros 2005).

The scene is set at daybreak, on a chilly, late summer or early autumn day, around the 2nd to the 3rd centuries AD. Of the five figures in the exhibition, one is a Roman merchant, the others are representatives of the Barbarians living outside Pannonia, two Sarmatians (a man and a woman), a Germanic man and a Barbarian woman wearing objects found in a grave in Veresegyháza, Hungary (Figs 3.1–3.6).

However, before we look at the reconstructions themselves, a brief account of their historical context is necessary. In the 1st century AD, when a new Roman province Pannonia was created in the western Carpathian Basin, the eastern regions of present-day

Hungary also came under the rule of new masters (see Map 3). This was the period, when the most western population of the Sarmatian tribal union, the Jazygians, migrated here from the Eurasian steppes. The Sarmatians, who belonged to the Iranian linguistic area, were closely related to the Scythians (see Gleba in this volume). The first Sarmatian wave invaded the territory between the Danube and Tisza rivers, which previously had been under the military control of the Dacians. Later, in the early 2nd century AD, the Sarmatians extended their rule to other Dacian domains on the eastern side of the Tisza, as a consequence of the triumphant wars of the Roman emperor Trajan over the Dacians. Germanic Quads migrated to the south-southeast from present day western Slovakia and became neighbours and brothers-in-arms of the Sarmatians. From the beginning, Quads were frequently mentioned together with the Sarmatians by Roman and Greek sources. The Vandals, another Germanic tribe, moved from today's Poland to the north-eastern corner of the Carpathian Basin during or shortly after the Marcomannic-Sarmatian wars (AD 168–180). The peaceful period after these wars led to prosperous commerce and trade between Romans and Barbarians in the Carpathian Basin (Istvánovits and Kulcsár 2005).

Costumes from archaeological excavations are very few and far between due to the geological and climatic conditions of the Carpathian Basin. That is why we needed to use different sources, *e.g.* archaeological, literary and pictorial, during the reconstruction of the five costumes.

Documenting the actual reconstruction process in writing, drawing and photographs was very important for us. As we used genuine archaeological finds – pins, buckles and beads – in these reconstructed costumes, we wished to mark their position on record accurately, for example by sewing small identification tags on the reverse side of the beaded embroideries with information such as inventory numbers and sites where the beads had been found; we also made drawings and photographs with the same data.

THE ROMAN MERCHANT'S COSTUME (FIG. 3.1)

The Roman merchant's costume was based on depictions on tombstones, the funerary stelae. Stelae from the western Roman provinces and present-day Hungary represent merchants wearing wide, unfitted tunics without girdles, with long sleeves reaching below the knee and a slightly shorter, sleeveless, hooded cape over it. Such figures often hold purses in their hands, which symbolize wealth and commerce.

The basic item of Roman provincial clothing was a loose tunic with long sleeves, which were either sewn into place or woven in one piece with the body of the garment. This unisex shirt, if it were ungirded, would reach down to women's ankles or to men's shins. The material of the merchant's tunic is of fine twill, dyed a purplish blue with alkanet (*Alkanna tinctoria*), which was also favoured by the Romans.

We are not sure if the exact classical name of the sleeveless, hooded cape was *caracalla* or *byrrus*. The difference between these two garments of Gallic origin is not known precisely. Their common characteristics are known from ancient literary sources: both were made of wool, were sleeveless and hooded, encircled the whole body and were sewn in the front. These two articles of outdoor clothing were more suitable for wearing over a tunic in bad weather than any other woollen rectangular cloak fastened by a pin on the shoulder. They were favoured by travellers, soldiers and peasants working in the fields (Wild 1963; 1964).

The *caracalla* was first mentioned by Cassius Dio in his *Roman History,* where Emperor Marcus Aurelius Severus Antoninus was described as frequently wearing this Gallic cape during his eastern military campaigns. He was, in fact, nicknamed *Caracallus* after his beloved garment (Cassius Dio LXXVIII, 3, 3). The emperor's robing habit was followed by many inhabitants of the Roman Empire, and the woollen Gallic capes with hoods became highly

Fig. 3.1: A Roman merchant and a Germanic man. (Courtesy of the Hungarian National Museum; Photo: András Dabasi)

popular and widespread garments from the 3rd century AD onwards. Due to their popularity and favourable preservation conditions, some examples survived in the arid deserts of Egypt and Nubia. These capes are from a geometric piece of cloth woven in shape on the loom: the rectangular section of the hood joins the centre on the straight line of a semicircular portion. The threads hanging from the curved edge of the textile have been twisted into a closing cord, after the cloth was taken off the loom (Granger-Taylor 1982).

We could get very little idea of the colours of the clothes from the tombstones themselves. For our Roman tradesman's costume, we had to use pictorial evidence from a Pompeian fresco representing a bread-purchasing scene, where one of the men has similar attire with a dark tunic without girdle under his natural-coloured cape. The only decorative element on his clothes is a narrow scarlet stripe on the hood.

The merchant's footwear (Fig. 3.2) is an exact copy of the ankle boot depicted on a bronze foot-shaped vessel from Szalacska, Hungary (Thomas 1963, 68–70, fig. 18). The cut and construction of the foot-wear, as well as the particulars of the decoration and lacing, can be easily followed on this metal find and also on Roman tombstones from the province of Germania. These ankle boots were open and laced up over the insteps. The inhabitants of the Roman provinces wore them over socks, together with

Fig. 3.2: Reconstructed footwear of the Roman merchant. (Courtesy of the Hungarian National Museum; Photo: Csaba Barbay)

a long-sleeved tunic and a hooded cape. The narrow, elegant soles with pointed toes were in use by AD 160 and, along with the toe caps on the uppers, rapidly spread all over the Empire during the 3rd century AD. Inside his boots of blackish calfskin, the Roman tradesman wears lilac coloured socks, which were reproduced on the analogy of a pair found in the military camp of Vindolanda, Britain. The two parts, the sole and the upper, of the original find had been recycled out of a well worn cloak.

We obtained further information on technological solutions not visible on these representations by inference, using the leather finds from excavated Roman settlements (Driel-Murray 1999, 40–41, 68–74). The Roman leather industry was highly developed, and of outstanding quality and specialisation. Innovations in leather processing methods, for example vegetal tanning, started to spread during the Roman Age, perhaps even with Roman influence. Thus, we used vegetally tanned soft calfskin to prepare the uppers and thick cowhide for the soles of the merchant's footwear. The multi-layered leather soles are studded with conical headed iron nails, as was often done by provincial shoemakers.

We seldom know the original colour of Roman footwear, because the arid zone of Egypt is the only location where leather finds have been discovered preserving the original shades relatively intact. Ancient authors write that the Roman leather industry was capable of producing many colours: red, purple, brown, yellow, white, gilded and black. According to their writings, black leather objects were quite common in Roman times (Lau 1967; Goldman 1994).

THE SARMATIAN COSTUMES

To reconstruct the costumes of the Sarmatians living in the Carpathian Basin, we made use of three kinds of evidence: data gathered from written sources, contemporary depictions created by the Sarmatians themselves or by the Romans, and archaeological finds. While the first two sources are mainly concerned with male costumes, the third one is highly significant in the case of women and children. Analysing the Roman pictorial representations of Sarmatian women and children, we saw that they were more schematic than representations on the Barbarian-made objects where mainly men were represented. We obtained further evidence for the reconstruction of the Sarmatian costumes from Scythian art, since Sarmatians were related to the Scythians and we could find similarities in their costumes. We had to handle this aspect very carefully, because costumes worn by a certain population vary over time and space.

We began reconstructing the Sarmatian female costume (Fig. 3.3) by selecting its material and colour. The most suitable starting point for us seemed to be the assemblage and reconstructed costume of a wealthy lady from the Sokolova Mohyla barrow of the 1st century AD, which was found in the Ukrainian steppe near South Bug (Kovpanenko 1986). The gold embroidery and appliqués on the purple and dark blue textiles from the burial mound indicate the shape of the costume. Both Ukrainian

Fig. 3.3: Reconstructed attire of a Sarmatian woman. (Courtesy of the Hungarian National Museum; Photo: András Dabasi)

and Russian scholars consider it a very significant find, and it also forms the basis of other reconstructions.

The eastern half of the Carpathian Basin was under Sarmatian rule from the 1st to the 5th century AD. We had to keep in mind the essential changes in the costume reflected by the archaeological evidence for the Sarmatian immigration from the steppes and their settlement in the Carpathian Basin during this period. As a result, we chose a period – the transition between 2nd and 3rd century AD – which was close in time to Sokolova Mohyla and was represented well by a relatively large amount of dated archaeological finds in the Carpathian Basin. The most datable accessories of the costumes are the pins or *fibulae*. As the archaeological evidence of the above mentioned period indicates, Sarmatian women only wore a single fibula on their costumes. The situation is, not surprisingly, similar in Sokolova Mohyla. Beside their utilitarian function in holding garments together, we can presume that they had decorative purposes. In some cases mineralized traces of a sewing thread in the corrosion of fibula-spring or beads mounted on the fibula pins are observed. Despite the fact that these objects are dated to a somewhat later time, we cannot reject the existence of this phenomenon earlier. The Sarmatians are the first in the Carpathian Basin who started to use buckles and belt-rings, the latter worn by women in the place of fibulae.

A great amount of gold appliqués sewn on the garments is a major characteristic of eastern Sarmatian costumes. Glass and semi-precious stone beads played the same role for the Sarmatians in the Carpathian Basin. In addition to being worn as necklaces and bracelets, the hundreds of beads often found around the ankles in women's graves are the most typical and specific characteristic of the Sarmatian female costume. In the burials, they were found as multi-rowed beaded decoration on trousers, on the lower hem of skirts, or on the soft boot-legs. Groups of beads on the waist and along the thigh, a unique feature of Sarmatian female burials, helped us to reconstruct a wide fabric belt, studded with glass beads and fixed by a silver or bronze belt-ring. Some of these later finds, however, had been made of iron with silver inlays.

Silk fabrics of varying thickness, obtained through trade, are known from Sarmatian burials, such as Sokolova Mohyla. We chose silk weft-faced tabby for the Sarmatian woman's garments. Her dark red dress is of a simple cut, extending down to the ankles. The neckline is round, while the sleeves narrow downwards. We designed beaded embroidery on the edge of the sleeves and the skirt, based on the grave finds (Fig. 3.4). The beads were made of glass and semi-precious stones. The bright colours of the beads dominate the whole ensemble and are very appealing to the eye. The motives of the embroidery applied on the hem of the reconstructed dress were based on a pattern stitched in gold thread from Sokolova Mohyla. We substituted the gold thread with colourful wool dyed with saffron, mallow and madder. Although the dress is covered with a loose coat, the rich ornamentation is still visible. The indigo-blue coat is open at the front and is much looser than the dress. Its sleeves are wide and elbow-length, thus the tighter sleeves of the dress are left visible. The lower part of the sleeves and the front part of the coat were decorated with colourful embroidery.

The accessories of the costume are earrings (fixed with a small hook and a loop), a

Fig. 3.4: The embroidery decorating the Sarmatian female dress. (Courtesy of the Hungarian National Museum; Photo: Csaba Barbay)

silver necklet, bracelets, and a leather purse, which is also decorated with beads.

There is no historical evidence which we could use to determine the exact shape and material of the Sarmatian woman's footwear and purse. However, grave finds attest that such items were decorated with semi-precious stone beads. Therefore, we tried to design a leather purse and boots which harmonized with the overall costume and which were able to display the eye-catching original chalcedony beads.

The soles of the boots are made of thick cowhide, the uppers are cut from soft calfskin. The outer and inner sides of the uppers were left open: this made it easier to put the boots on. The footwear can be fastened by leather strings lacing the sides together through cut holes. The purse is made of a front and a back part. The latter includes the bottom of the bag, the belt loop and the flap. The chalcedony beads were sewn onto the strap hanging from the flap, thus they also serve as counterweights for closing the purse.

As mentioned earlier, we are much more knowledgeable about the appearance of Sarmatian men than of women. They appear, for example, on the battle scenes of the Sarmatians against Roman armies on the frieze of the Emperor Trajan's Column in Rome, or on many funerary stelae found in Crimea, especially in present day Kerch, the ancient

Pantikapaion of the Bosporan Kingdom. The warriors depicted on these stelae and the figures in the tombs' frescoes provided us with much information. In recent years, many silver vessels have turned up in southern Russian excavations, for instance in Kosika. The decorations on these vessels represent the battles and hunts of Sarmatian men.

While the attire of Sarmatian men is better represented than that of women in a wide range of ancient depictions and descriptions, the archaeological information from male graves is more scanty. Therefore, we created the male costume mainly on the basis of the pictorial representations, and less on the archeological finds of the Sarmatians. This was completed by comparisons with data on the related Scythians, because pictorial depictions of them are more abundant (see Gleba in this volume). These portrayals are visible on the gold- and silverware made possibly by Greek goldsmiths, who decorated their precious works with stories from Scythian mythology and scenes from combat and horse-riding.

A red-dyed leather coat of eastern origin, or more precisely its remnants, was the basis for our choice of the colours for the Sarmatian male costume. It was found in a princely or royal burial in Porohy, in the Ukraine (Simonenko and Lobai 1991). As plenty of Sarmatian finds, mainly scabbards and headgear, had traces of red colour, we had reason to believe that red was popular amongst the Sarmatians. Heavy draperies, *e.g.* brocade, interwoven or embroidered with gold, were also quite frequently used by the Sarmatian elite.

The reconstructed costume of the Sarmatian man (Fig. 3.5) is composed of three elements: an undershirt, a coat and a pair of trousers with loose-fitting legs. The orange woollen trousers of a diamond twill are dyed

Fig. 3.5: A Sarmatian man's costume. (Courtesy of the Hungarian National Museum; Photo: Csaba Barbay)

with madder. An embroidered pattern runs along the outer side of the trouser legs. It can be observed on several Scythian gold relief representations that a decorative band runs along the edge of their kaftans (see Figs 2.7 and 2.8 in Gleba in this volume). It might have been made of fur or a decorated piece of ribbon. The fabric of the reconstructed woollen kaftan is a felted herringbone twill. It was hemmed with a narrow, brick-coloured band made from the fabric of the trousers and also decorated with embroidery.

The Sarmatian man's shoes with clasped straps are well-known both from archaeological contexts in Hungary and from depictions of the Sarmatians and of other related ethnic groups, such as Scythians and Persians. This was an ankle-length boot with strapping and saddler's seam over the instep. In certain cases, a vertical seam is also visible on the side of the boots. The uppers of the reconstructed boots were created from soft calfskin, and the soles of thick cowhide. A bronze distributor divides the strapping, which runs along the ankle towards the sole of the boot. This holds the spur, which is fixed at the front with a silver buckle and strap-end.

THE COSTUME OF A GERMANIC MAN

Tacitus is probably the classical author most frequently cited in connection with the attire of Germanic men. He informs us that their costume consisted of a big, rectangular, multi-coloured cloak (*sagum versicolor*), a tunic and trousers, and that their costumes were not loose as those of the Sarmatians and the Parthians, but tight, emphasizing their figure (Tacitus *Germania*, 17). Apart from the written sources, our reconstruction work was also based on Roman depictions, especially on the Column of Marcus Aurelius in Rome, bronze statuettes and the costume items found in 1863 in the Thorsberg Bog, present-day Schleswig-Holstein, Germany, consisting of a long-sleeved tunic, tight trousers and a large rectangular cloak (Schlabow 1976). This assemblage of finds has been considered to be the embodiment of the typical Germanic, male costume ever since. Tacitus' description and the pictorial data mentioned above are complimented by the analysis of certain burial assemblages. The dead were buried in their clothes, and the mineralized textile remains of their costume on the metal accessories indicate that the deceased wore woollen clothes similar to the Thorsberg costume: a fine shirt, a coarser tunic over it, trousers and the checked cloak, which was fringed on one side and had a tablet-woven band on one or on all other sides (Maik 2001). The size of these cloaks very often was over 1.5 by 2.5 m. The checked pattern, rooted in the Pre-Roman Iron Age, belonged to the traditional motif system of the Germanic and Celtic tribes. Their Roman conquerors looked on it with some disdain. Nevertheless, with the expansion of the Roman Empire, the checked cloak spread to the Eastern Mediterranean.

We did not intend to recreate an exact copy of the Thorsberg cloak (Schlabow 1976, 63–65, Mantel 12), as we didn't wish to imply that items identical to this exceptional piece were generally used in the Carpathian Basin and all over Europe. We wanted to design a very similar cloak, which was different in detail (see Fig. 3.1). For example, we added green to the blue shades of its twill. The wide decorative band of our cloak was woven using no less than 50 square tablets. According to the analysis of the textile finds from archaeological contexts, the cloaks were usually woven together with their decorative tablet-woven bands on a warp-weighted loom. However, examples with bands sewn on are also known (Maik 2001).

The long-sleeved tunic and the trousers of our Germanic man have also been created based on the examples from Thorsberg. The small cord fasteners under the armpits are the special elements of the shirt: its back and front can be fixed tying them together (Schlabow 1976, 69–71, Kittel 1). A colourful, tablet-woven band of 10 tablets decorates the tunic's neck opening and wrists. In the case of the stocking-like, tight pair of trousers which covered the toes as well, its delicate tailoring is remarkable (Schlabow 1976, 76–77, Hose 1). Its twelve component pieces have been cut out from one piece of cloth of at least 1.2 by 1.4 m. There are no seams on the sides, one seam runs along the back, open only at the calves, which could be tightened by 8-8 strap fasteners. Six strap holders were put on the waistband, which was formed by folding back the textile.

The original source for our copy of the Germanic man's footwear was a man clad in a cloak and trousers found at Damdorf, Germany. For our reconstruction, we made the man's shoes from a single piece of cowhide tied over the toes by thongs cut from the same piece of the leather. The technical solution that was used to make the thick cowhide more flexible is remarkable: an openwork design was created by small longitudinal cuts incised along on a large surface of the upper outer side (Hald 1972, 54–57, fig. 49). Foot-shaped vessels of burnt clay representing similar footwear testify that this relatively simple type of footwear was quite popular among the prehistoric populations preceding the Romans, and that it was worn not just outside the Roman Empire but was also widespread among the Roman provincial populations. The thick cowhide had to be soaked in water for a whole day to make it possible to form it into shape. When the leather was soft enough, we folded the upper over the instep on a last, and then fixed them with the thong. It was compressed to this form using bones and a hammer. After this procedure, the leather holds its shape but loses fats. The use of beeswax is recommended to compensate for this. We smoothed down the edges of the thick cowhide with wax and a bone tool to obtain its worn appearance.

THE COSTUME OF A BARBARIAN WOMAN

The metal accessories of a Barbarian woman belong to a set of finds from a female burial discovered during a rescue excavation in Versegyháza (Mesterházy 1986). The grave contained different Barbarian elements: a silver Dacian torc, a pair of Germanic bracelets and a characteristic Sarmatian belt. These were completed by a silver Roman *fibula*. The multi-cultural variety of these accessories encouraged us to dress this figure in a costume which may have been commonly worn in the Carpathian Basin (Fig. 3.6).

According to Roman pictorial evidence, such as the column of Emperor Marcus Aurelius and Roman tombstones, the indigenous women living in the Carpathian Basin wore a *peplos*-like gown, in the form of a simple tube of cloth with the back and front held together at the shoulders by a pair of pins or – according to the words of Tacitus – spikes, but occasionally just sewn together (Becatti 1957; Garbsch 1965). Such garments were generally worn in Roman Age Europe and probably have their roots in the pre-Roman Iron Age. They are documented by provincial Roman sculptures, by archaeological textile finds from Danish bogs and by mineralized textiles on the surface of metal objects from graves. The analysis of Germanic burials in Poland indicates that women were dressed in such tubular garments made of wool, and that they wore a long-sleeved bodice of finer wool under it. Their attire was completed by an elegant rectangular cloak, similar to those worn by men (Maik 2001).

The Barbarian woman's dress was prepared from a rectangular piece of woollen twill 1.3 by 2 m in size. It was sewn together under the armpit to create a tube. The length of the gown was modified by two belts. Her underwear was a long-sleeved, ivory-coloured woollen shirt. We fastened her chequered cloak, similar to that worn by the Germanic man, with the original silver *fibula*, which was found in the Verseghyáza burial. As the

Fig. 3.6: A Barbarian woman. (Courtesy of the Hungarian National Museum; Photo: Csaba Barbay)

dominant colour of the Germanic man's costume is blue, we thought it appropriate that his female counterpart should wear clothes of the same colour. She also wears a pair of socks that have been prepared by the needle-binding technique. Her footwear (Fig. 3.7) was based on bog finds from Northern Germany (Hald 1972, 51, figs 46–47). They were created from a single piece of cowhide sewn on the heels and tied by thongs over the toes. They have an openwork design. Although the original colour of the find could not be established, we dyed the leather dark brown to match the rest of her costume.

Fig. 3.7: Reconstructed footwear of the Barbarian woman. (Courtesy of the Hungarian National Museum; Photo: Csaba Barbay)

CONCLUSIONS

The aim of the organizers of the exhibition "On the Borders of East and West" was to display not only the invaluable archaeological finds stored in the Hungarian National Museum, but also to present the possible context and aspects of their usage. We prepared the above-described reconstructed costumes to fit certain requirements (date, time and context) of the pre-determined scenario of the exhibition. At the same time, we relied on literary, iconographic and archaeological evidence to reconstruct visually how these peoples could have looked like in the past.

The main question for us was: How do we make a visual reconstruction of a group of people for the exhibition visitors? Our reconstruction of these five figures is only one among several possibilities. For instance, we do not believe that all Roman merchants had the same type of attire regardless of age, gender or social status. While several possible archaeological solutions for the exhibition existed, in our reconstruction we attempted to weave together the available archaeological data with the requirements of the exhibition.

All reconstructions are characterized by duality and ambiguity: as they are the product of their own age, summing up our current knowledge of the contemporary dress-code in ancient societies, they reflect both our past and present. The reconstructions answer some of our questions, but they also raise new ones.

ACKNOWLEDGEMENTS

Márta Csökmei (hand-weaver), Anikó Horváth (leather accessory designer), Loránd Olivér Kovács ("Germanic man"), Myrtill Magyar ("Barbarian woman"), Mónika Polka ("Sarmatian woman"), Zoltán Rostás ("Sarmatian man"), János Skorutyák (blue-printer), Dr. Zsuzsa Pluhár (for madder roots) and István Weigl (for the iron hobnails) deserve our special thanks for their invaluable help, expertise and enthusiasm during our collaboration on the reconstruction.

BIBLIOGRAPHY

Further information about the concept of the exhibition is available in Istvánovits and Kulcsár (2005) and in Rezi Kató and Vasáros (2005). There is a valuable summary of the archaeology of the Roman Age Carpathian Basin in Visy (2003). For Roman fashion and clothing in general, see Croom (2000). An essential work on western provincial dresses is Wild (1968). Summaries of Sarmatian clothing in the Carpathian Basin are in Vaday, Istvánovits and Kulcsár (1989) and Istvánovits and Kulcsár (2001).

In this chapter, the following works have been used:

Becatti, G. (1957) *Colonna di Marco Aurelio*. Milan, Editoriale Domus.

Croom, A. T. (2000) *Roman Clothing and Fashion*. Stroud, Tempus Publishers.

Driel-Murray, C. van (1999) Die römischen Lederfunde. Das Ostkastell von Welzheim, Rems-Murr-Kreis. *Forschungen und Berichte zur Vor- und Frühgeschichte in Baden-Württenberg 42,* 11–109.

Garbsch, J. G. (1965) Die norisch-pannonische Frauentracht im 1. und 2. Jahrhundert. *Münchener Beiträge zur Vor- und Frühgeschichte XI.*

Goldman, N. (1994) Roman Footwear. In J. L. Sebesta and L. Bonfante (eds) *The World of Roman Costume*. Madison, WI: University of Wisconsin Press, 101–129.

Granger-Taylor, H. (1982) Weaving Clothes to Shape in the Ancient World: The Tunic and Toga of the Arringatore. *Textile History* 13 (1), 3–25.

Hald, M. (1972) *Primitive Shoes. An Archaeological-Ethnological Study Based upon Shoe Finds from the Jutland Peninsula*. Copenhagen, National Museum of Denmark.

Istvánovits, E. and V. Kulcsár (2001) Sarmatians through the eyes of strangers. The Sarmatian warrior. In E. Istvánovits and V. Kulcsár (eds) *International Connections of the Barbarians of the Carpathian Basin in the 1st–5th centuries AD. Proceedings of the international conference held in 1999 in Aszód and Nyíregyháza*. Aszód and Nyíregyháza.

Istvánovits, E. and V. Kulcsár (2005) Barbarians of the Roman Age (turn of the millenium – early 5th century AD). In E. Garam (ed.) *Between East and West. History of the peoples living in the Hungarian land 40,000 BC–804 AD. Guide to the Archaeological Exhibition of the Hungarian National Museum*. Budapest, 106–114.

Kovpanenko, G. T. (1986) *Сарматское погребение I в. н. э. на Южном Буге*. Kiev, Naukova Dumka.

Lau, O. (1967) *Schuster und Schusterhandwerk in der griechisch-römischen Literatur und Kunst.* Bonn, Phil. Diss, 1967.

Maik, J. (2001) Recent textile finds of the Roman period in Poland. In P. Walton Rogers, L. Bender Jørgensen and A. Rast Eicher (eds) *The Roman Textile Industry and its Influence: a Birthday Tribute to John Peter Wild.* Oxford, Oxbow Books, 105–112.

Mesterházy, K. (1986) Frühsarmatenzeitlicher Grabfund aus Veresegyháza. *Folia Archaeologica* 37, 137–161.

Rezi Kató, G. and Zs. Vasáros (eds) (2005) *Kelet és Nyugat határán. A Magyar Nemzeti Múzeum állandó régészeti kiállítása.* On the Borders of East and West. The Permanent Archaeological Exhibition of the Hungarian National Museum. Budapest.

Schlabow, K. (1976) Textilfunde der Eisenzeit in Norddeutschland. *Göttinger Schriften zur Vor- und Frühgeschichte 15.*

Simonenko, A.V. and B. I. Lobai (1991) *Сарматы Северо-западного Причерноморья в I в. н. э.* Kiev.

Thomas, E. B. (1963) Ornat und Kultgeräte einer Sol- und Luna-Priesterin aus Pannonien. *Acta Antiqua* 11, 49–80.

Vaday, A., E. Istvánovits and V. Kulcsár (1989) Sarmatian Costume in the Carpathian Basin. *Klio* 71, 107–114.

Visy, Zs. (ed.) (2003) *Hungarian Archaeology at the Turn of the Millennium.* Budapest, Dept. of Monuments of the Ministry of Cultural Heritage.

Wild, J. P. (1963) The Byrrus Britannicus. *Antiquity* 37, 193–202.

Wild, J. P. (1964) The Caracallus. *Latomus* 23, 532–536.

Wild, J. P. (1968) Clothing in the North-West Provinces of the Roman Empire. *Bonner Jahrbucher* 168, 166–240.

Chapter 4

A Weaver's Voice: Making Reconstructions of Danish Iron Age Textiles

Anna Nørgaard

In this chapter, the author, a professional hand weaver, gives an account of her reconstruction of an Iron Age costume from Huldremose for the National Museum of Denmark. In the process, she also gives us an insight into her thoughts on the art of reconstruction.

Keywords: Huldremose, craft, prehistoric weaving, loom, reconstruction, copy.

As a child, I often wondered why ancient costumes and their reconstructions were always brown. And of course, that's exactly how clothes look after they have spent centuries buried in the ground – brown and a bit drab. More than 50 years ago, many researchers thought that textiles from the Bronze Age and Early Iron Age were made from wool mixed with deer hair. Extensive research, better microscopes and improved scientific analytical techniques have helped us to build up a far greater knowledge base about the textiles of the past. We now know that the long, coarse hairs used in these textiles were outer hair from the sheep of the time. Today, we are also able to tell whether the wool had once been white, naturally pigmented in various shades of brown, grey and black, or whether it had been dyed with natural colouring agents.

This knowledge has multiplied our options for reconstructing garments as they looked in ancient times, before they decayed and turned brown. However, this means that many more decisions must be made during a reconstruction. It also means that we need to consider the difference between a copy and a reconstruction.

MAKING A RECONSTRUCTION – THE WHAT, WHY AND HOW

To me, a copy is an exact replica of the original. If, for instance, you are working with a piece of metallic jewellery that you can make a wax cast of, enabling you to cast an object that is identical to the original, down to its smallest irregularities, then you have a copy.

Using this definition of a copy, it is impossible to produce an exact copy of a piece of ancient textile, for which the original yarn would have been spun on a spindle and woven on a loom without a reed. It can only be a reconstruction. How close you want it to be to the original has to be a matter of judgement in each individual case. Should the yarn for the reconstruction be hand-spun? If so, should it be spun on a spinning wheel, even though the original yarn would have been spun on a spindle? Is it possible to find people who are capable of spinning yarn the way the original yarn was spun? If so, will it be worth the financial cost to have that type of spinning, compared to machine-spun yarn? Often, it is a question of money. The more skilled labour involved and the more precise the technique, the more expensive it becomes.

It is also necessary to consider what the reconstruction is going to be used for. Is the costume or textile destined for an exhibition, where it will be behind glass? Or will the public be allowed to touch it? Will it be used for teaching, theatre or role playing?

Then, there is the question of exactly what is to be reconstructed? If it is a costume, do you want to make an imitation of what has been excavated from the ground, retaining the colours it has assumed after many years in the earth? Or do you want to reconstruct the costume as it would have looked at the time of its deposition into the ground?

Many excavated costumes have suffered a great deal of wear and tear, and marks have been left in them by pins, jewellery or belts. Sometimes, they have been patched with a fabric of different quality from the original, or their hems have been repaired with a sewing thread different from the original. These traces of wear and tear tell a story of their own, including how the costume was worn. Perhaps it was remade for a new owner at some stage in its life, or the fabric had been used for something else before it was turned into a costume. A reconstruction of such a costume can be very exciting, but also complicated to make.

Another possibility is open to us today, which is to reconstruct the costume as it looked when it was brand new and worn for the first time. By considering colour and fibre analyses, we can deduce the quality and colour of the garment when it was new. This type of reconstruction gives the public a completely different, more realistic impression of the textiles and costumes of the past, compared to imitations of the brown textiles unearthed from the ground.

The ancient costumes we have found would have been woven and sewn to fit the user's height and girth. We need to ask whether the reconstruction should be made to precisely the same measurements as the original. For example, if it is to be used for teaching purposes, is it justifiable to change the pattern so the costume fits a modern child? We are generally larger today than people were in ancient times, and that includes children.

This is an important issue, because you can easily end up changing the costume's style, both in terms of shape and fabric quality, if you do not possess knowledge of ancient clothing customs and weaving techniques. I have seen reconstructions of garments very unlike the originals, because the decision had been made to spin the yarn on a spinning wheel or spindle, without taking into account the fact that the people who spin the yarn today are not practised craftspeople like those who spun the yarn for the originals, and who would have grown up using that specific tool.

Generally, yarn used in ancient weaving was very uniform in thickness, hard spun, and with the same number of twists per centimetre throughout the yarn. This last point can be particularly difficult to stick to for an unpractised spinner and, if the number of twists is not even, it can result in bumps in the woven fabric. If the yarn is too thick and uneven, the fabric can easily look as if woven by an inexperienced weaver, and that was seldom the case with ancient textiles.

The choice of whether a reconstruction should be woven on a warp-weighted loom or on a loom with a tubular warp can also yield very different results. Neither loom has a reed, so there is nothing to keep the warp threads in place, other than the skill of the weaver. It requires plenty of practice to avoid the weaving in these looms from shrinking, or becoming narrower along the way. In some of the archaeological Iron Age textiles we can see that this was also a problem for weavers of that time. In some cases, it can therefore be better to buy a ready-spun yarn and do the weaving on a horizontal loom with a reed, depending on how skilled a craftsperson you are.

When I am asked to reconstruct a piece of prehistoric textile or costume for a museum, I always begin by asking what it will be used for and what the budget is. If the garment is to be displayed in a glass case and will never be touched, for example, you can sew some of the inner seams by machine, saving money and energy for the more visible details.

If a reconstruction is to be used to show what people wore in the past (for example to demonstrate what the Vikings wore to resist the cold and rain when they sailed from Norway to Greenland), the clothes should be sewn and woven as close to the original methods as possible. If, on the other hand, the reconstruction is to be used for role playing or theatre, where the focus is on the story rather than the clothes, then the costumes do not need to be perfect down to the smallest detail.

If the costume is to be used for teaching school children for example, is it acceptable for it to be sewn on a machine? I have discussed this with many people, and I often hear the opinion, that if the fabric has been machine woven, why not also sew the garment by machine, when the children won't be able to identify the difference anyway? However, if children cannot see the difference between a machine seam and a hand-sewn one, it is because they have never been shown the difference. Some machine-woven fabrics look hand woven, but I have never come across a sewing machine that can make sewing look like prehistoric stitching.

RECONSTRUCTION OF A COSTUME FROM HULDREMOSE

In May 1997, an exhibition opened at the National Museum of Denmark in Copenhagen featuring some of the museum's textiles from the Iron Age and the Viking era in Denmark (Fig. 4.1). The idea of the exhibition was to display in the same room the original garments in closed display cases, alongside uncased reconstructions of them, so the public could

Fig. 4.1: Opening of the exhibition at the National Museum of Denmark in Copenhagen in 1997 showing the reconstruction uncased and behind it, the original in a closed display case. (Photo: Kit Weiss)

almost touch them. The aim was to give people a sense of how the costumes would have looked when they were new.

The reconstruction work was carried out already in 1991–1992. Thus, the work was done on the basis of the latest scientific research available at the time. New research is produced constantly, so if I were to reconstruct the same costume in the future, I would do so from a different knowledge base.

One of the original costumes, which was found in Huldremose, consisted of a skirt with waistband, a scarf and two skin capes (Hald 1980) (Figs 4.2, 4.3, 4.4, 4.5). The reconstruction of this costume should have been as similar to the original as possible in terms of material, spinning and weaving, so that museum visitors could compare the two. This, at least, was the plan.

Threads were sampled from the original textiles (in the first instance, the skirt and scarf), and samples sent to a laboratory in York, England (Walton 1991). Today, the skirt looks as if it would have had a checked pattern in two shades of brown. However, the analysis showed that the yarn in the stripes, which today look light brown, were spun from completely white wool, with no trace of plant or other colouring agent. The yarn in the darker stripe turned out to have been spun from wool with a moderate amount of pigment

Fig. 4.2 (left): The reconstruction of the Huldremose skirt and scarf. The scarf may have been worn as a headscarf. (Photo: Roberto Fortuna)

Fig. 4.3 (right): The reconstruction of the inner cape. (Photo: Roberto Fortuna)

Fig. 4.4 (left): The reconstruction of the entire costume. (Photo: Roberto Fortuna)

Fig. 4.5 (right): The reconstruction of the entire costume. (Photo: Roberto Fortuna)

particles, and the laboratory concluded that it must have been a light brown wool, also non-dyed from a naturally brown sheep.

The scarf is also woven in a checked pattern, but includes at least three different shades. In this case, the samples showed that the checks were formed from yarn spun from white wool, as well as yarns of light brown and dark brown wools. There was no trace of dyeing here either.

The wool in both the skirt and scarf corresponded to the wool from a type of mouflon sheep, which has a very soft undercoat and little kemp. This came as no great surprise, as the mouflon was the most common sheep of the time. However, it is a problem today to find wool of corresponding quality.

The colour was another problem. Natural brown wool fades easily. Because of this, spinning mills normally over-dye brown wool, in order to prevent complaints from customers. Furthermore, the budget did not allow for hand-spun yarn.

After receiving samples of yarn and speaking with a number of yarn companies and spinning mills, we settled on two options: a Faroese yarn or a Norwegian yarn. The yarn from the Faroe Islands contained far too much hair, however, and would have made the fabrics very stiff, which the originals were not. On the contrary, the latter would have been soft to wear, with a beautiful drape.

The Norwegian yarn was a single-thread knitting yarn called Stobi, which is spun from pure Norwegian wool, and it was available in the right shades of natural brown. The yarn was loosely spun but a second spinning on a spinning wheel made it suitably firm. The actual wool quality (the fibre) was a bit thicker than in the original, but it was the closest we could obtain.

The Huldremose Skirt (National Museum of Denmark, Mus. No. C 3473)

The original skirt was 87 cm in length and 271 cm in circumference. First and foremost, all the threads in the original were counted in both warp and weft directions, to give an overview of the pattern. Overall, there is a pattern in the checks, but during the counting of the threads, a number of irregularities emerged. For example, where there should have been a stripe of eight threads in the warp, there would suddenly be six. Wherever there was an irregularity, it was always divisible by two. This tells us that the warping of the skirt was done by the loop method, where two threads were warped on the loom at a time.

In general, the weft also follows a regular pattern, but there are significantly more irregularities here than in the warp. Here too, all the differences are divisible by two. This must have been due to the weavers always having the shuttles lying at the waistband side when they were not in use. After making a mistake in the weave, it is possible that the weavers did not discover it until a point when it would have been too much work to unpick it all. It is also possible that the occasional mistake was not that important to them. And on the whole, the mistakes are not particularly visible.

The question arose whether the mistakes should also be copied, since the pattern is so regular. As this reconstruction was being created as a comparison to the original, it was decided to copy the mistakes as well. It also added a bit more excitement and fun to the project.

Another interesting observation is that, in the originals, sometimes, two weft threads cross one another, suggesting that two people were weaving simultaneously. These criss-crosses are not regular, however, so the pair clearly did not work together throughout the whole weaving process.

The further I advanced with the work, the more I felt at one with the people who had originally sat at the loom weaving the cloth. I could almost feel the way the original weavers sat and chatted, so engrossed in their conversation that they forgot to count the weft, so that suddenly there were too many or too few threads in a stripe.

The skirt was probably woven on a loom with a tubular warp. An important characteristic of a textile woven on a loom with a tubular warp is the warp lock. The lock is the thread around which the loops of warp thread are laid, alternately from one side then the other. The weaving then starts with the warp-lock and ends there again. This results in a piece of fabric which can be either tubular, if the lock remains in place, or square, with a finished edge on all four sides if the lock is pulled out. If the weaver does not weave all the way down to the lock, it results in loops of warp thread at the beginning and end of the cloth.

In the Huldremose skirt, the loops on one edge have been folded inwards on the back of the skirt and sewn down, so it is difficult to measure their length. But they are very short. On the opposite end, the loops are somewhat longer – approximately 3 cm – and here, the loops have been used to braid a very beautiful edge. The fabric has then been sewn together again with double thread and some long herringbone stitching.

It might seem strange to weave a tubular skirt with a waistband, in a matching check the whole way round, and then to remove the lock and sew the skirt together to create a closed skirt again. The reason might have been that the weavers gave up working on the last centimetres of the warp, which is the most difficult piece to weave on a loom with a tubular warp. Perhaps the loops at the start had also become a bit too big and irregular, so they chose the easiest and best solution.

Based on my experience of other reconstructions, I knew it would take at least 100 hours to weave the skirt on a loom with a tubular warp. This would be very expensive, so it was decided to weave the reconstruction on a modern horizontal heddle loom. The question now became one of whether the skirt could be woven on such a loom without that being noticeable.

The original skirt has a very special waistband in warp-faced tabby, which was woven at the same time as the skirt. At the bottom of the skirt, there is a tubular woven tabby hem over 14 warp threads. This tubular edge and the waistband make the two selvedges of the fabric on the loom.

The original skirt had been woven with an average of 7–9 threads per cm in both warp and weft. For the reconstruction, we chose a reed 40/10 with two threads per dent – in other words, eight threads per cm. This is slightly less than the original, and since a weave always shrinks a little during weaving, the resulting recon-struction was, in fact, a couple of centimetres shorter than the original. As the length of the original skirt mentioned here is an average length, this was still acceptable.

As I had an old reed with a suitable density, I cut a piece of it off so that, when it was lying in the batten, but attached to the warp for the skirt, the warp of the waistband was out of reach of the reed (Fig. 4.6). The advantage of this was that the reed did not wear down the warp threads, as these were very close – 58 in 3.5 cm, of which the outermost 14 threads created a tubular woven hem. The warps for the waistband were heddled on the 1st and 3rd shafts.

The tubular-woven selvedge at the bottom presented no problems. Here, the threads were heddled on the 2nd and 4th shafts. When the shuttle with the weft thread came out

Fig. 4.6: The warp-thread of the lining lies outside the reed, so that it does not get frayed by it. (Photo: © Anna Nørgaard)

of the fabric, it went through all the threads; but when it was brought back again, the shuttle was not inserted into the fabric until after the tubular-woven edge. The selvedge was, by this means, pulled together into a ring and as it was only woven in every second weft, it became automatically woven in tabby.

The skirt was woven with two shuttles with white and brown yarn in a 2/2 twill, while the waistband was woven in warp-faced tabby with two weft threads in each shed. In other words, there are twice as many wefts in the actual fabric as in the waistband. This means that a weft in the waistband does not always continue down through the material in the skirt, but instead is met by another, which comes up through the fabric. The two wefts are twisted around each other and the one that emerged from the fabric is inserted back into the fabric in a new shed. The weft from the waistband adopts a waiting position until the weft from the fabric again comes back to the waistband. Now, the two weft threads are again twisted around each other and are led back where they came from in the fabric and waistband respectively. When a colour is changed, the weft with the new colour goes directly from the waistband down through the fabric, and the other weft thread remains lying between waistband and fabric until it is needed in the next shed. This process was not systematically implemented in the original, so during the reconstruction we had to make the changes as they came, but this presented no problems when using the horizontal loom.

After the skirt was removed from the loom, the fabric was folded under where the weaving had started and sewn down with backstitch, just like in the original. The other side was slightly more complicated; this was where the braided hem was to be. But we succeeded in braiding a corresponding hem from the remainder of the warp threads, so that the resulting outer side looked like the original (Fig. 4.7). On the inner side of the skirt, the fact that the warp has been cut off and does not end in loops is visible, of course, but this was unavoidable. It was also acceptable, given that the costume was being made for an exhibition where its back would not be visible.

The skirt was then sewn together with long herringbone stitches in double yarn, like in the original. Then the skirt was placed in clean water to remove the stiffness from the fabric which occurs when the yarn has been stretched in a loom. It took a total of 60 hours to reconstruct the skirt.

Fig. 4.7: The braided edge of the skirt, where the weaving ended. (Photo: ©Anna Nørgaard)

Compared to the original, which was woven on a loom without a reed, the reconstruction inevitably has a far smoother, more regular surface. It might also be said that it is not as 'lively' as the original, in which the stripes vary a little in breadth. I think the original skirt from Huldremose is incredibly smooth in its overall appearance, and is the most beautiful and most professionally manufactured piece of textile I have seen from the Iron Age.

The Huldremose Scarf (The National Museum of Denmark, Mus. No. C 3474)

The original scarf is 50 cm wide, with the length varying between 133 cm on one side and 141 cm on the other, excluding the fringes. This is because the weaving became skewed along the way. The average density of threads for the warp and the weft are the same as for the skirt.

The original description of the find reads: "Around the neck was found the headscarf, fastened with the pin still in situ. The scarf was cut into two pieces when it was removed, as the pin was not noticed until later, and one side of the scarf was stuck under the left arm" (National Museum of Denmark, Unpublished Report).

When the find was made on the 21st May 1879, it was probably unthinkable for a woman to go outdoors without a headscarf or hat. If this piece of fabric was supposed to be a headscarf, it is understandable that it could have slid down around the neck – but why would it be fastened with a pin under the left arm? The size is also rather unusual for a headscarf.

After experiments with different ways of wearing this garment, it became clear that it had to be a form of shawl or blouse, which covered the right shoulder and was fastened under the left arm, leaving the left shoulder bare. This interpretation became more probable when we started to work with the leather capes, as the innermost cape turned out to be sewn with a shoulder pattern for the left shoulder. This is described more fully in the following discussion of the reconstruction of the capes.

The scarf has a closed warp indicating that it could have been woven on a backstrap loom or a loom with a tubular warp, and it has loops at both ends. At the point where the weaving starts, the fringes are only approximately 1 cm long, but where the weaving ends, there are double fringes of between 1.5 cm and 5 cm.

When I prepared to weave the reconstruction of the scarf, it became clear that I would not obtain these loops of warp threads if I wove it on a horizontal loom, so I decided to use a backstrap loom (Fig. 4.8). The work took 55 hours in total, including second spinning, warping and the twisting of the loops at the end.

The chequered pattern in the reconstruction was woven in three shades, like the warp and weft pattern that emerged from the analysis, but the same quality of yarn was used throughout. This varied from the original, for which a thicker, white yarn was used towards the end of the weave.

As I sat weaving the scarf, I had the clear impression that the original had not been woven with the same expertise as the skirt. The yarn in the original scarf had also been spun far more unevenly. Furthermore, there are many mistakes in the distribution of both

Fig. 4.8: The scarf was woven on a backstrap loom. (Photo: Roberto Fortuna)

warp and weft threads. As in the skirt, the irregularities in the warp are at intervals of two threads, but the wefts often have an uneven number, which would be due to the placing of the shuttles when they were not in use. Three shuttles with one colour each were used for this particular pattern, so two shuttles would have been passive at the same time. During the reconstruction it became clear that it was practical to place one of these shuttles on each side of the work. The passive weft yarn was hidden inside the tubular woven selvedges, which helped make the sides stronger. This is also visible on the original.

I was anxious to see whether I could get the same skewed effect in the weaving at the end as in the original. This happened more or less of its own accord, as I, like the original weaver, obviously have a tendency to knock the weft harder together on my right hand side. It was not as skewed as the original, however. It is precisely this sort of factor that makes it impossible to produce an exact copy of a piece of textile. No two people weave in exactly the same way.

While I was weaving, the wefts were pressed together with a narrow sword beater, but I also used a comb beater. It was difficult to beat the weave together because it was impossible to wield the sword beater, due to the too small distance between the woven fabric and the heddles. It is always like that with a backstrap loom but, since there were no problems getting the right density of the wefts, the choice of tool was not so significant.

Two leather capes from Huldremose (National Museum of Denmark, Mus. No. C3471 and C3472)

The leather capes are almost completely preserved but have been patched and repaired on many occasions in ancient times. Today, it is difficult to identify when the various repairs and mending were done. As a consequence, I sought the help of a professional cloth cutter who also knows about the history of clothing and 'primitive' cuts: Hanne Meedom, associate professor at the Day and Evening School in Skovlunde, in Denmark.

Together, we drew all the small details and patches on tracing paper and Meedom sewed a reconstruction of each cape in canvas, so that we had models to work from. This also afforded us an opportunity to test different ways of wearing the capes.

Some people have interpreted the inner cape (C3471) as a sleeveless blouse, because it has two slits at the top by the neck. The find report states: "This leather garment, which was found worn right next to the skin, had to be cut up on one side when being removed" (National Museum of Denmark, Unpublished Report).

The slits are, however, only 15 cm and 17 cm long. These would make very small armholes, and there were definitely no sleeves. When we decided instead to sew the slits together, a cape with a shoulder pattern appeared, in which the two slits became two shoulder seams. The opening for the arm was then revealed to be at the right shoulder.

It is difficult to say whether our interpretation is correct. On the face of it, it might seem impractical if one arm (in this case, the left) was hidden under a cape in everyday use, but we do not know if this was the original owner's daily clothing, or what her daily life was like. The cape has been repaired and patched many times, and was well worn before being used as a shroud.

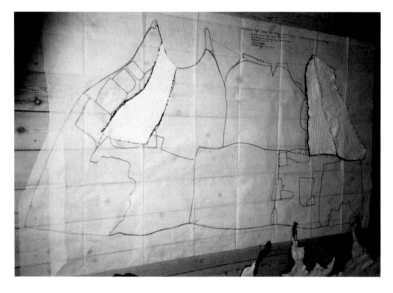

Fig. 4.9: The pattern for the inner cape with three cut out skins. (Photo: © Anna Nørgaard)

Originally, however, the inner cape consisted of 11 small animal skins sewn together. While we were measuring it up, skin samples from the original were sent to be analysed by the National Museum of Denmark's leather conservator, Vivi Lønborg Andersen. Along with these, we sent samples from every breed of sheep we could find. Andersen concluded that the animal skins that had been used in the inner cape were closest to a sample of Persian lambskin.

I contacted a furrier, who showed me 11 Persian lamb-skins. When I put each pattern piece of the cape on a lambskin, it was surprising to see what an exact fit they were (Figs 4.9–4.11). Persian lambskin is lamb-skin from karakul sheep. The lambs are born with short, soft, shiny, very curly fur, with the curls tightest on the back and usually receding down towards the legs. It was once rumoured that the coats of Persian lambs came from unborn or aborted lambs. This is not the case, of course, but it is true that as a

Fig. 4.10: Some of the small lambskins each with its pattern piece. (Photo: © Anna Nørgaard)

rule, the lambs are slaughtered before they start to need food other than their mother's milk, because the fur changes character at that point.

It was interesting to see how the curls on the skins used in the original cape were mainly concentrated around the middle of the individual pieces. On many, the curls disappeared towards the corners. This confirmed for us that the cape had been sewn from the hides of quite small lambs.

If you want to tan a skin, the animal must be skinned within an hour of its death, unless you freeze the carcass. I now contacted everybody I knew who had sheep, irrespective of breed, and asked them to freeze any lambs that died within the first few weeks of birth, so I could collect their skins later and tan them.

I ended up with quite a nice collection of lambskins in all sizes, colours and qualities. The most interesting thing was the extent to which the quality of the skins varied, even within the same breed, ranging from some that looked like Persian lambskin to others that were completely curl-free. It proved impossible for me to collect enough skins of the same quality as the cape, however, so we ended up buying the 11 Persian lambskins. It resulted in an extremely soft cape, with fine, curled lambswool on the inside, next to the body. It is difficult to tell whether the Iron Age people had done as I did, tanning skins from lambs that had died, or whether they had used lambs that had been slaughtered, either for food or specifically for their skins. Perhaps someone specialising in Iron Age farming will one day have an opinion on that.

Fig. 4.11: One of the largest pattern pieces which perfectly fits the lambskin. (Photo: © Anna Nørgaard)

The skin used on the outer cape (C3472) turned out to be of a rougher quality than the inner cape, although it is still quite fine, with short, curly wool. The sample from a Gotland sheep was the closest to the hides that had been used in this cape. The colour analyses showed that the wool in both capes was from brown sheep, with the exception of a white piece on the back of the shoulder of the outside cape.

I contacted the Association of Gotland Sheep Breeders, who put me in touch with Arwid Carlsson near Borås in Sweden. He believed that the Gotland sheep were originally brown, and he has managed to breed (or revert to) a brown Gotland fur, by crossing a Gotland sheep with a brown Spelsau. We used three of these brown skins, together with

*Fig. 4.12: The individual pattern pieces for the outer cape before they were sewn together. (Photo: ©
Anna Nørgaard)*

part of a white one, to make the whole cape (Fig. 4.12). Samples were also taken from the
thread that had been used to sew the capes together, but for me, it was already obvious
that they had used a form of non-spun sinew thread perhaps from the back muscle of a
horse.

Textile scholar Margrethe Hald writes, however, that some Iron Age capes were sewn
with leather thread (Hald 1980, 280). For this reason, I did attempt to sew with both
tanned and untanned skin thread, but when the hide was cut as thin as the original sewing
threads, it was not strong enough to sew with, so I would dispute that theory. I also tried
flax thread, but it looked completely wrong in comparison to the original. Finally, I
succeeded in procuring a manufactured synthetic sinew thread from Lapland, which the
Saami use in their crafts.

CONCLUSIONS

Today, there is a great demand for reconstructions of prehistoric costume, both for
teaching purposes and for displaying in museums. Museum visitors like to see human
beings from the past come alive, through sight and touch, and perhaps even by trying to
live as their ancestors did. In this chapter I have described some of the problems that
occur when producing reconstructions, and the questions that have to be asked before
and during this work process. The reconstruction of the Huldremose costume was used as

an example because of its completeness and complexity. In my collaboration with museums and archaeologists, it is my experience that much new knowledge is gained through reconstruction. As a craftsperson, I can see and understand details of textiles which provide new insight into how they were made.

ACKNOWLEDGMENTS

The first draft of this chapter, including the quotations from the National Museum of Denmark's Unpublished Report, was translated from the original Danish by the University of Copenhagen's Translation Centre.

BIBLIOGRAPHY

Crowfood, G. M. and H. Ling Roth (1974) *Hand Spinning and Woolcombing*. Reprinted by Ruth Bean from the original Bankfield Museum Notes, Halifax, England.
Fränkel, J. (1960) *Rauchwarenhandbuch, mit Sachregister in 7 Sprachen. Die Tiere im Pelzhandel*. Privately printed by Karl Schahl, Lörrach-Stetten.
Hald, M. (1980) *Ancient Danish Textiles from Bogs and Burials*. Copenhagen, National Museum of Denmark.
Historisk Arkæologisk Forsøgscenter Lejre (1985) Rapport vedrørende vævning af en kopi af Huldremose-peplosen, november 1985, Nr. 05/85. (A report in Danish from the Lejre Experimental Centre on weaving a copy of the Huldremose peplos).
Historisk Arkæologisk Forsøgscenter Lejre (1986) Rapport over forsøg af vævning af en peplos på Tekstilværkstedet, november 1986, Nr. 56/86. (A report in Danish from the Lejre Experimental Centre on weaving a peplos at the Textile Workshop).
Hoffmann, M. (1964) *The Warp-Weighted Loom*. Oslo, Universitetsforlaget.
Ling Roth, H. (1977) *Studies in Primitive Looms*. Reprinted by Ruth Bean from the original Bankfield Museum Notes, Halifax, England.
Matter, H. E. (1968) Karakul, Breitschwanz und Persianer, *Schriften für Pelz- und Säugetierkunde „Das Pelzgewerbe"*, 4–6/1967, Hermelin-Verlag.
National Museum of Denmark (*n.d.*) Unpublished Report NM: II j. nr. 364/96=39/97.
Walton, P. (1991) *Examination of Wool and Tests for Dye in Textile Samples from Huldremose, Denmark*. Unpublished Report, 19th May 1991, Textile Research Associates. Presented to the National Museum of Denmark in Copenhagen.
Wild, J. P. (1988) *Textiles in Archaeology*. Aylesbury, Shire Publications.

Chapter 5

Iconography and Costume from the Late Iron Age in Scandinavia

Ulla Mannering

In this chapter, new ways of interpreting and evaluating costume are introduced through the analysis of iconographic sources, among others gold sheets from the Late Iron Age in Scandinavia. These sources contain invaluable information about prehistoric dress.

Keywords: gold sheets, iconography, gender, Bornholm, Late Iron Age, Scandinavia.

Prehistoric textile and costume research has a long tradition in Scandinavia. Due to some very favorable preservation conditions, Scandinavia possesses a large and varied collection of textiles from different contexts. However, the evidence for prehistoric costume is not equally well preserved in all periods. In the Late Iron Age period, 5th–11th centuries AD, most textile finds are very fragmented and it is difficult to extract general characteristics about Scandinavian Late Iron Age costume based on these finds alone.

At Bornholm Museum on the Danish island Bornholm, two reconstructed life-sized costumes are exhibited (Figs 5.1 and 5.2). They are placed in the same room as the rich find of gold sheets from the Sorte Muld site on Bornholm, dated to the 6th–7th centuries AD (Watt 2004). Gold sheets are a purely Scandinavian phenomenon and the vast majority of the more than 2900 recorded gold sheets come from this location. The function of the gold sheets is not known but they are tiny images of humans or human-like figures stamped, scratched into or cut out of thin gold sheets, often the size of a fingernail or approximately 1 cm^2 (Fig. 5.3).

The above mentioned costume reconstructions are meant to be seen as a possible mirror image of the human models used by the Late Iron Age goldsmiths who made the gold sheet figures, and they exemplify how the gold sheet images can be combined with the textile finds from this period. The result has a great popularizing effect but it is definitely not always easy to combine iconography with archaeological material. There are many pitfalls both in the registration and interpretation of the iconographical material. In prehistoric society, we only have very little or indirect knowledge about the mentality,

Fig. 5.1: Reconstructed costume of a female gold sheet figure, Bornholm Museum (Courtesy of Bornholm Museum; Photo: Allan Juhl)

Fig. 5.2: Reconstructed costume of a male gold sheet figure, Bornholm Museum (Courtesy of Bornholm Museum; Photo: Allan Juhl).

social structures or praxis that governed the production of these images and therefore there is a great risk of misunderstanding or misinterpreting intentions and signals passed on to us. Nevertheless, seen from an archaeologist's perspective, this is far too informative a source to disregard just because it is difficult to work with or because of the risk of doing something wrong. In archaeology, there are no absolute truths, only the material culture itself and the knowledge gained by many different researchers throughout the

Fig. 5.3: Gold sheet figures from Sorte Muld in Denmark (Photo: courtesy of Martin Stoltze / Bornholm Museum)

years. But, before information about iconography and costume can be connected in a scientific and successful way it is necessary to explore the iconographic sources systematically and in a source critical way.

Iconography is not a new source in ancient or modern costume research. On the contrary, many different researchers have used it successfully in their studies (see *e.g.* Hald 1980; Schlabow 1976; Wilson 1924, 1938; Wild 1968, 1985; Vogelsang-Eastwood 1992, 1993). It is, however, still rare to see systematic studies of iconographic costumes in their own right. In Scandinavian prehistoric archaeology, iconography has primarily been used to support conclusions about characteristic features known from the archaeological textile and costume corpus. In my doctoral thesis, I have tried to make up for this lacuna by integrating the iconographical costumes in the discussion of Scandinavian Late Iron Age costume tradition (Mannering 2006).

ICONOGRAPHY AND COSTUME IN THE LATE IRON AGE

At the beginning of the Late Iron Age, we see the development of an independent Scandinavian iconography containing humans and human-like figures, and, for a period of more than 600 years, we can follow the expression and development of these figures in the depictions. They are found on a varied range of artefacts such as picture stones, runic stones, wood carvings, tapestries, gold sheets, jewellery, weapons and a wealth of single artefacts like gaming pieces, earspoons, small figurines and the like. In some cases, the image is part of the decoration, in other cases, the image is the object. Some are monochrome, some are polychrome, but they all seem to share the same idiom.

In my research I selected and worked with iconographical costumes from five different sources: gold sheets, bronze sheets from helmets, bracteates, a selection of jewellery and tapestries. The aim was to see how and why these different artifacts alone and in combination can contribute to existing knowledge about costume in iconography and about costume in prehistoric society (Mannering 2006).

As I chose to investigate images from different contexts with different dates and use, the first challenge was to develop a method of recording the different characteristics in the images that can bridge these differences. On the one hand, the recording method had to contain an appropriate number of characteristics without being too detailed and thus blurring the perspective. On the other hand, the method had to keep a balance between norm and variation without distorting or over-interpreting the data. Initially this work resulted in the creation of an iconographic costume typology which can be used to compare different sources with different interpretations, uses or contexts (Fig. 5.4). In this way, it is easy to identify the different shapes in the images, to add new types to the scheme and, eventually, to use this format on other materials (Mannering 2006).

The selected study material comprises more than 1,000 different representations of male and female costumes on more than 500 different objects. Based on an overall evaluation of the images selected for the analyses, the iconographical costumes can be grouped in a uniform and simple system of different costume shapes and combinations.

Gold sheets contain the largest and most varied number of costumes and costume combinations. Gold sheet figures can either display one person or two people facing each other. Approximately a quarter of all gold sheets are clearly dressed and in spite of their small size, it is surprising how many details can be distinguished. It was undoubtedly of greatest importance that the clothing could be recognised, and great effort was made to make the dress decipherable (Mannering 2004).

Women generally wear more layers and longer garments than men. The typical female figure is characterized by an ankle-length dress; long hair may be tied in a knot at the back of the head. Sometimes the figures also wear different jewellery. In many cases, the women also wear a cloak that can either be closed in front, or rests on both shoulders, as can be seen in the figures to the right hand side in Figs 5.5 and 5.6. Males generally wear fewer layers of garments than females. The basic male costume consists of a tunic that may reach the knees and perhaps trousers with wide or narrow legs, as can be seen in the figures to the left of Figs 5.5 and 5.7; and men often wear their hair short. In some cases, but not as often as with the women, men also wear cloaks, as in the figure to the left in Fig. 5.6. However, male cloaks are always closed on the shoulder, which creates a different iconographical shape than in the case of their female counterparts. This does not mean that the shape of the garment was different. Rather, it demonstrates that the garment was worn in a different way depending on the sex of the wearer.

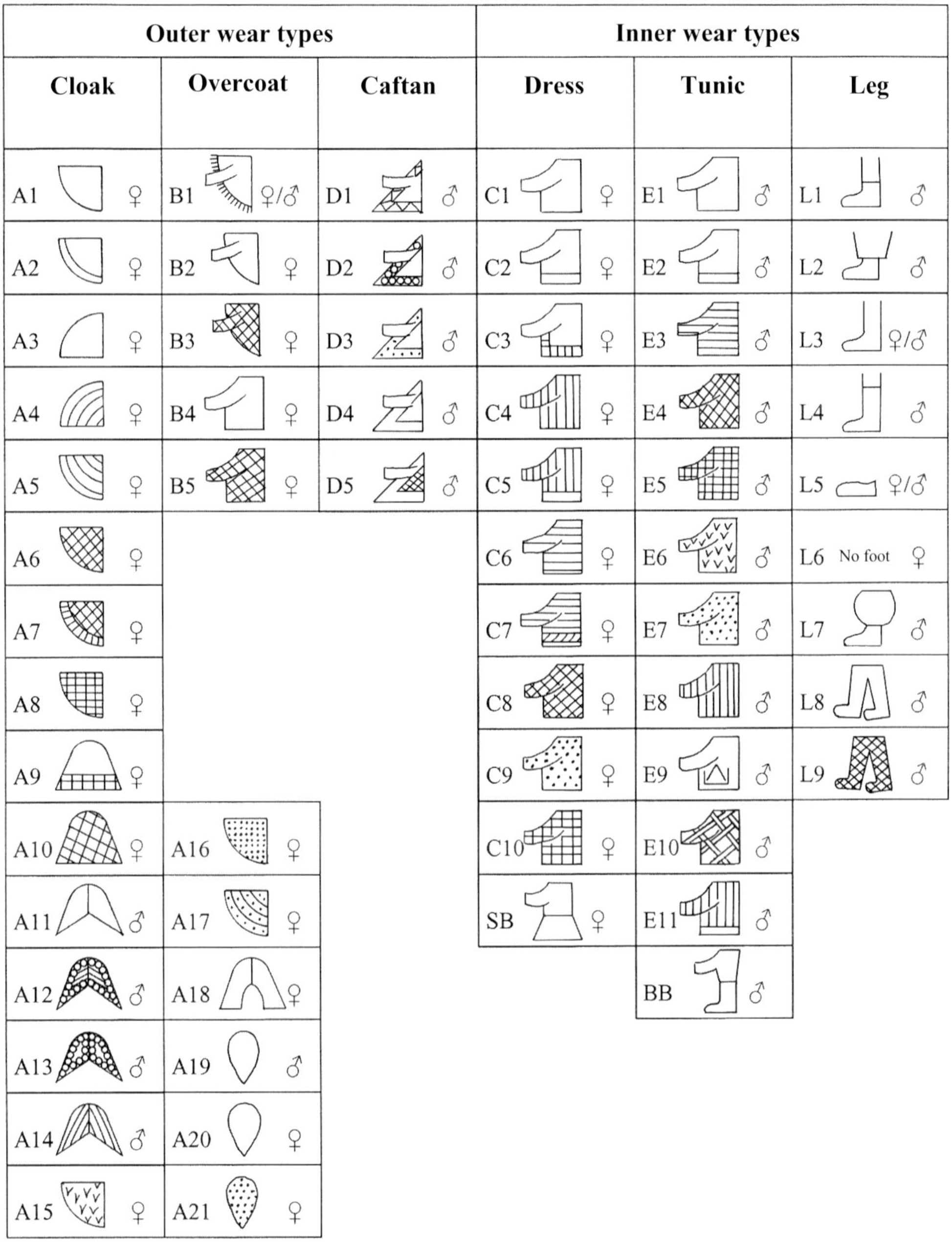

Outer wear types			Inner wear types		
Cloak	**Overcoat**	**Caftan**	**Dress**	**Tunic**	**Leg**
A1 ♀	B1 ♀/♂	D1 ♂	C1 ♀	E1 ♂	L1 ♂
A2 ♀	B2 ♀	D2 ♂	C2 ♀	E2 ♂	L2 ♂
A3 ♀	B3 ♀	D3 ♂	C3 ♀	E3 ♂	L3 ♀/♂
A4 ♀	B4 ♀	D4 ♂	C4 ♀	E4 ♂	L4 ♂
A5 ♀	B5 ♀	D5 ♂	C5 ♀	E5 ♂	L5 ♀/♂
A6 ♀			C6 ♀	E6 ♂	L6 No foot ♀
A7 ♀			C7 ♀	E7 ♂	L7 ♂
A8 ♀			C8 ♀	E8 ♂	L8 ♂
A9 ♀			C9 ♀	E9 ♂	L9 ♂
A10 ♀	A16 ♀		C10 ♀	E10 ♂	
A11 ♂	A17 ♀		SB ♀	E11 ♂	
A12 ♂	A18 ♀			BB ♂	
A13 ♂	A19 ♂				
A14 ♂	A20 ♀				
A15 ♀	A21 ♀				

Fig. 5.4: Iconographic costume typology. (From Mannering 2006)

The costumes on the gold sheets also show a sleeved overcoat which can be divided into male and female types (Fig. 5.4; see also Figs 5.5 and 5.7). A specific male overcoat, also called a kaftan, is iconographically characterized by diagonal front lines indicating that it was open in the front (Fig. 5.8). This specific type is restricted to single representations and thus never occurs together with representations of women.

On the bronze sheets from warrior helmets, only male depictions occur. However, the range of costumes is very similar to those seen on the gold sheets (Hauck 1978). This type of depiction is more narrative in its format than the gold sheets, and here we often see horsemen or fighting warriors clad in kaftans. As these pictures have a clear military connotation, it is possible to interpret the kaftan as an attribute of the warrior and this could also explain why men wearing this type of garment are never found combined with women on the gold sheets.

Unlike the costumes on the gold sheets and the bronze sheets from helmets, the costumes of the figures displayed on the bracteates are neither very clear nor detailed, and in many cases we may wonder whether the figures are dressed at all. Bracteates are gold pendants inspired by Roman coins and medallions and they predate the other selected objects (Axboe and Kromann 1992). Obviously, in these depictions the costume is not as important as other parts of the picture. Thus, there seem to be an iconographical conflict

Fig. 5.5: Drawing of double-figured gold sheet from Slöinge in Sweden. (From Mannering 2006)

Fig. 5.6: Drawing of double-figured gold sheet from Hauge in Norway. (From Mannering 2006)

in transforming the Roman layout into a locally understandable format. Nevertheless, the bracteates are important in costume research forming an intermediate stage towards a more independent Scandinavian iconography where the costumes play such an important role.

Dressed figures occurring in jewellery represent a very heterogeneous group of artefacts, which in most cases have been used as pendants (Holmqvist 1960). They are found throughout a long period of time, which makes it difficult to treat them as a unit. In general, depictions of women and female costumes resemble the gold sheets to a large extent: most often they wear dress and cloak. The male costume is composed of the same elements as on the gold sheets and bronze sheets from helmets: tunic or blouse and trousers in different lengths and widths; but in this category there are no men dressed in kaftans.

The tapestries are few, as a group, but each tapestry contains many figures, since in most cases they display complete narrative scenes (Christensen *et al.* 1992; Franzén and Nockert 1992; Christensen and Nockert 2006). In general, the tapestries contain mainly male depictions and the few females are stylized to an extent that makes costume studies difficult. The male costume consists in most cases of wide breeches and a short cloak or very long wide tunic, quite unlike the garments seen in the other categories. This group is

Fig. 5.7: Drawing of double-figured gold sheet from Helgö in Sweden. (From Mannering 2006)

Fig. 5.8: Drawing of single-figured gold sheet from Sorte Muld in Denmark. (From Mannering 2006)

dated to the latest part of the examined period and it can be noted that changes in the selection of costumes depicted and in the role of the female in iconography take place during the selected period (Göransson 1999).

CONCLUSIONS

Having studied more than 1,000 costumes in five different artifact categories, it is striking that it is possible to recognize the same costumes and costume combinations in almost all categories. The makers of each artifact category seem to have had both a realistic idea of how costumes were supposed to look like and, at the same time, a fixed range and way of combining these costumes. Small but significant variations and changes in the costumes can be observed from one group of artifacts to another, and these changes may perhaps be linked to changes taking place in prehistoric costume. For instance, the same tendency in iconography as in the archaeological textile record to differentiate male and female costumes is evident. The development of the male costume, which becomes wider and longer towards the end of the period, shows how the iconographical costumes reflect their archaeological counterparts. There can be no doubt that the images show realistic costumes from their time, albeit filtered through artistic canons. However, we also gain information from the images, which cannot be recognized in the archaeological textile record, and *vice versa*.

The purpose of the depictions was not to show contemporary fashion but high class figures or icons, which are clad in contemporary costume. Seen from this perspective, the iconographical costumes can play an important role in costume research; and with this in mind it should be possible to use these costumes as a substantial supplement to the often all too fragmented textile remains, as has been done at Bornholm Museum.

A fascinating aspect of using iconography as a source in its own right is that the images tell their individual story of the prevalent attitude towards body and dress, providing information that can be difficult to extract from other artefacts or even from the costume finds themselves. When the sources are looked at and analysed systematically, the iconography forms a useful base for further discussion of costume design, gender, social status and symbolism.

BIBLIOGRAPHY

Axboe, M. and A. Kromann (1992) DN ODINN P F AUC Germanic "Imperial Portraits" on Scandinavian Gold Bracteates. *Acta Hyperborea* 4, 271–305.
Christensen, A. E., A. S. Ingstad and B. Myhre (1992) *Osebergdronningens grav*. Oslo, Schibsted.
Christensen, A. E. and M. Nockert (eds) (2006) *Osebergfunnet. Vol. IV. Tekstilene*. Oslo, Kulturhistorisk Museum, University of Oslo.
Franzén, A. M. and M. Nockert (1992) *Bonaderna från Skog och Överbogdal och andra medeltida väggbeklädnader*. Stockholm, Kungl. Vitterhets Historie och Antikvitets Akademien.

Göransson, E.-M. (1999) *Bilder av kvinnor och kvinnlighet . Genus och kroppsspråk under övergången till kristendomen*. Stockholm Studies in Archaeology 18. Stockholm, Stockholm University.

Hald, M. (1980) *Ancient Danish Textiles from Bogs and Burials*. Copenhagen. National Museum of Denmark.

Hauck, K. (1978) Bildforschung als Historische Sachforschung. Zur vorchristlichen Ikonographie der figuralen Helmprogramme aus der Vendelzeit. In K. Hauck and H. Mordek (eds) *Geschichtsschreibung und Geistiges Leben im Mittelalter*. Cologne, Bohlau, 27–70.

Holmqvist, W. (1960) The Dancing Gods. *Acta Archaeologica* 31, 101–127.

Mannering, U. (2004) Dress in Scandinavian Iconography of the 5th–10th centuries A.D. In J. Maik (ed.) *Priceless Invention of Humanity – Textiles,* NESAT VIII. Acta Archaeologica Lodziensia Nr. 50/1. Łódź, 67–74.

Mannering, U. (2006) *Billeder af dragt. En analyse af påklædte figurer fra yngre jernalder i Skandinavien*. PhD. Dissertation, University of Copenhagen.

Schlabow, K. (1976) *Textilfunde der Eisenzeit in Norddeutschland*. Neumünster, Wachholtz Verlag.

Vogelsang-Eastwood, G. (1992) *Patterns for Ancient Egyptian Clothing*. Leiden.

Vogelsang-Eastwood, G. (1993) *Pharaonic Egyptian Clothing*. Studies in Textile and Costume History vol. 2. Leiden, Brill.

Watt, M. (2004) The Gold-Figure Foils ("Guldgubbar") from Uppåkra. In L. Larsson (ed.) Continuity for Centuries. A Ceremonial Building and its Context at Uppåkra, Southern Sweden. Uppåkrastudier 10. Acta Archaeologica Lundensia, Series 8, No. 30. Lund, 167–221.

Wild, J. P. (1968) Clothing in the North-West Provinces of the Roman Empire. *Bonner Jahrbücher* 168, 166–240.

Wild, J. P. (1985) The Clothing of Britannia, Gallia Belgica and Germania Inferior. *Aufstieg und Niedergang der Römischen Welt*. Teilband II 12, 3, 362–422. Berlin.

Wilson, L. M. (1924) *The Roman Toga*. Baltimore, Johns Hopkins Press.

Wilson, L. M. (1938) *The Clothing of the Ancient Romans*. Baltimore, Johns Hopkins Press.

Chapter 6

Tools, Textile Production and Society in Viking Age Birka

Eva B. Andersson

Investigation of textiles is important when we discuss costume practice, gender and social status. Studying raw materials, tools and techniques used in textile production provides valuable knowledge of the organisation of textile craftsmanship as well as the economic and cultural role of textiles in a society. While there are textile finds from this period, most of them are fragmentary. Thanks to textile scholars, however, we have acquired information, not only on raw materials, but also on the techniques used to manufacture textiles. In contrast, textile tools are ubiquitous in settlements and some prehistoric textile techniques, such as spinning and weaving on a warp-weighted loom, have a tradition lasting to this day and we can therefore understand how and for what purposes they were used. With all this information woven together we have a good opportunity to elucidate textile production and its importance in society. This chapter focuses on textile production in the Viking Age port of trade Birka, where Sweden's largest assemblages of Viking Age textile tools and textiles have been found.

Keywords: tools, Birka, Viking Age, handicraft, women, production, society.

The Viking Age trading port of Birka is situated on Björkö, a small island in Lake Mälaren (see Map 4) in east Sweden. The region is rich in antiquities from the Iron Age and Viking period. During the Viking Age, settlements expanded rapidly in this region. Based on the amount of graves and cemeteries, the number of settlements has been estimated at about 1000 farms in 800 AD and 4000 farms in 1100 AD (Ambrosiani 1985, 103).

Birka is famous because it is the earliest known 'town' in Sweden with evidence of both international trade and specialised craftsmanship. It consisted of a settlement area of around 7 ha, the so-called Black Earth area, of which only 6–7% has been excavated, and approximately 3000 graves (Ambrosiani and Eriksson 1996, 43). Birka has been dated principally on the basis of grave finds. According to the latest results, the main period of Birka spanned a period of just 220 years (750–970 AD). The population of Birka has been estimated at 700–1000 individuals in the early period and around 1500 in the late phase (Ambrosiani and Clark 1991, 157).

Of the estimated 3000 graves, around 1160 have been excavated. Of these, 551 are cremation burials, 94 are so-called chamber graves and the rest are inhumations. The chamber graves are very rich in preserved textiles, jewellery and other valuable items. The social structure of the Birka population has been discussed by several scholars (*e.g.* Arbman 1955; Gräslund 1980; Hägg 1983). They have compared the grave finds in relation to Rimbert's *Vita anskarii* that states that there were chieftains, rich merchants, craftsmen, ordinary people and slaves in Birka. Gräslund sums up her analysis of the graves by observing that:

> The grave goods in some inhumation and cremation burials indicate great wealth, others (some chamber-graves) demonstrate by their construction that the deceased belonged to a high social stratum despite the absence of rich grave goods. It is likely that all these were the burials of chieftains and their families as well as merchants, either local or from other Scandinavian areas or from countries outside Scandinavia (Gräslund 1980, 86).

The people of Birka could not have existed in a place as isolated as Björkö without any connection to the mainland. A precondition for the existence of the place is that it attracted merchants and craftsmen on the one hand and the population of the mainland on the other. Although the inhabitants of the site were in contact with contemporary North European towns, they would have been highly dependent on the mainland to satisfy their basic needs for food, timber, firewood and raw materials. In particular, there was a great need for raw materials for textile production. Large quantities of wool and, possibly, flax and hemp were required in order to cover production for household requirements (Andersson 2003, 63).

THE TEXTILES FROM BIRKA

The textile finds from Birka are of great importance for our knowledge of Viking Age textiles. In the 1930s, Swedish textile scholar Agnes Geijer did pioneering work with her systematic analysis of these finds. While the textile material from the graves is very fragmentary, it gives a good picture of different types of costumes; there is also evidence for cushions and carpets or hangings used to furnish the graves (Geijer 1938).

Geijer divided the fabrics into four groups: (1) coarser fabrics mostly woven in tabby; (2) patterned twill fabrics of high quality; (3) ribbed fabrics and other tabby weaves of fine quality and (4) simple twills. She was convinced that most of the fabrics of high quality were imported to Birka because of their uniformity. Geijer assumed that it was impossible to produce these types of textiles locally especially with wool from the Scandinavian sheep (Geijer 1938). Later, Inga Hägg suggested that the linen fabrics were also imports (Hägg 1974, 100). According to Geijer and Hägg, the only types of fabric that were produced in Scandinavia at this time were of the coarser qualities. This assumption has been accepted by most textile scholars although the origin of these textiles has been widely discussed over the years (*e.g.* Geijer 1938; 1965; 1980; Hoffmann 1964; Ingstad 1980; 2006; Bender Jørgensen 1986; Hägg 1987.

We know from the textile finds and written sources like the Icelandic sagas that textiles, tapestry and sails were of great importance for the Vikings. In the Sagas, we read about men and women wearing different types of garments such as shirts, cloaks, trousers, shoes and gloves. Costumes are differentiated and specified as high-status, military costumes, simple clothing, dresses that were worn out, magic garments, textiles given as gifts, and textiles for exchange and trade. Most of the textiles were found in the very rich chamber graves, therefore, the finds of textiles do not represent the general needs of the people of Birka. Even if the many archaeological textile finds in Birka are unique, they do not give a complete picture of all the textiles the inhabitants needed and produced.

RAW MATERIAL, TEXTILE TOOLS AND TECHNIQUES IN BIRKA

It must be acknowledged from the outset, that when working with the interpretation of raw material and tools, there are several problematic issues to contend with, in regard to our sources. Analyses of archaeological textiles confirm that different raw materials were used, yet there is no exact knowledge of for instance, the varieties of sheep that existed at the time. It is uncertain when the cultivation of a plant like flax was introduced to Scandinavia, and we do not know for certain what the flax looked like, or how it was grown.

Textile tools made of organic material are usually not preserved, so we do not know to what extent they were used. Spindle rods, looms, but also shuttles, reels, and swifts have vanished, and even objects made of other materials like iron can rust away and perish. What we have are tools made of stone, bone and clay such as spindle whorls and loom weights. However, even if some information is missing, we can still obtain a great deal of knowledge from the preserved tools and textiles.

Raw material

The major raw materials used in textile production in Birka, as in the rest of Scandinavia, were wool and flax. Wool seems to have been the most important, but at the same time, it must be borne in mind that linen rarely survives, and its lack is perhaps above all a problem of preservation. The latter is also the case for nettle and hemp fibres.

Forests and heaths could be used as sheep pastures; the islands in the archipelago would also have been good for grazing. In the medieval provincial laws there are detailed rules on grazing rights and customs on the islands in Lake Mälaren (Szabó 1970, 70). In the osteological material, one can see that sheep rearing increased in Sweden and, above all, on the islands in the Baltic Sea in the 1st millennium AD, in contrast to the development in the rest of Northern Europe, where the relative proportions of bones of cattle and sheep remained the same as before (Pedersen *et al.* 1998, 367).

The osteological analysis of animal bones from Birka and the hinterland shows that sheep products such as wool and mutton were imported there from the mainland.

Both flax and hemp were cultivated in the Iron and Viking Age in the Mälaren valley. Most pollen diagrams also show a great expansion of hemp cultivation in the period AD 600–1000 (Hansson and Dickson 1997; Pedersen *et al.* 1998, 382).

Wool and wool preparation

Sheep in the Viking Age were probably smaller than today's sheep, and it is difficult to determine how much wool could be obtained from one animal. Icelandic sources from the early 19th century state that an ewe could yield 1–1.25 kg of washed wool and a wether between 1.75 and 2.5 kg of wool (Adalsteinsson 1990, 286).

The wool was plucked or cut from the sheep. There are around 100 archaeological finds of shears from the Birka burials, and knives are one of the most common items in the Birka graves. Not all of these finds, however, would have been suitable for wool shearing.

A sheep has different kinds of wool: the fine-fibred and curly wool nearest the skin; the hair, which is longer, coarser, and stronger than the wool; and kemp, which is coarse and stiff and easily broken. The fibre properties of wool can vary greatly within the same type of sheep (Andersson 1999; 2003). The difference may be due to factors such as the food available to the sheep, but there can also be individual differences within one and the same group. There is also a great difference in the coarseness of wool fibres depending on which part of the sheep the wool comes from. Wool from the thighs, for example, is much coarser and longer than wool from the sides and shoulders. This differing structure of the wool was utilized in textile production. The long hairs were used when strong thread was needed, for example, in the warp.

The sorting of wool into different groups of fibre and the preparation of the wool for spinning are two important stages if the work is to proceed as easily as possible and if the yarn is to be evenly spun.

The wool can be spun immediately after it has been shorn or plucked from the sheep, but usually it is first teased by hand or combed with the aid of wool combs. In Birka several comb teeth have been found, but there are no finds of complete wool combs (Andersson 2003, 89).

When the long hairs are to be separated from the wool, two wool combs are used (Fig. 6.1). First, one of the wool combs is filled three-quarters full with wool. The wool is then combed with the other comb from the top and the sides until all the long fibres are well combed and lie parallel, sticking out beyond the sides of the tool. The long hairs are then drawn out of the wool comb by hand in a long strip of fibres, the hairs then lying parallel and ready for spinning. It is virtually impossible to achieve 100% separation between hair and underwool, and there is always a certain amount of underwool left in the yarn, just as there is always a certain amount of hair left in the wool. The underwool that remains in the combs can, of course, be used for spinning as well, but with this wool one spins a different type of thread since the fibres are much shorter.

After combing, the fibres are rolled into a rolag and during the spinning this is either held in the hand or attached to a stick, known as a distaff. The distaff can be held under the arm or attached to the lining of the skirt.

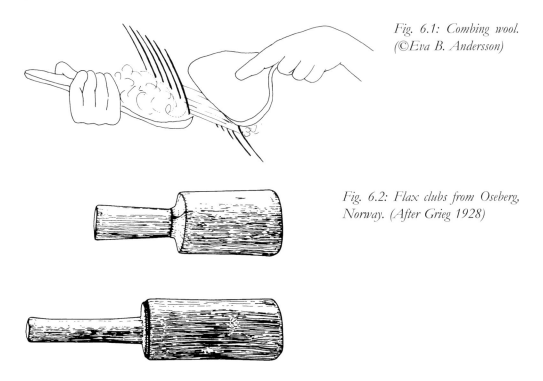

*Fig. 6.1: Combing wool.
(©Eva B. Andersson)*

*Fig. 6.2: Flax clubs from Oseberg,
Norway. (After Grieg 1928)*

Flax and its preparation

When flax is ripe it is pulled up by the roots and the seeds are rippled. The flax then has
to be retted. The stems can either be placed in water or spread on a dewy ground. The
moisture assists in the process of dissolving the pectin found between the bunches of
fibre in the bark and the stem. The next stage is breaking, when a wooden club is used to
break up the stem and the bark which are to be separated from the fibres (Fig. 6.2). After
that, at least in historic times, the flax was scutched with a broad wooden knife, which
scraped away the last remains of stem and bark. Finally the fibres are hackled, or combed,
with the aid of a tool which, like a wool comb, has long iron teeth.

No flax preparation tools in Birka or its surroundings are preserved, which is not
surprising since they were mainly made of wood. On the other hand, there are some finds,
from both the burials and the settlement area, of smoothing stones and even three
smoothing boards. These items have been interpreted as tools to make fine linen fabrics
smooth and shiny. They are made of glass or stone but a smoothing tool made of bone
could also have been used. To smooth a fabric, it was stretched on a hard surface, known
as a smoothing board, and then rubbed with the bone or the stone. The finds of smoothing
stones in Birka are mainly made of glass and there are also many bone finds that could
have been used for the same purpose. These tools do not constitute direct evidence for the
manufacture of linen on the site. But as mentioned before, there are several finds of linen

textiles and also evidence that flax was cultivated in the region, so it is most likely that people produced linen for textile production in the Mälar area and in Birka.

Other textile raw material

Another raw material that could have been used in Birka is hemp. Hemp is related to flax but its fibres are coarser. In the analysis of plant remains found in sediment just outside the Black Earth at Birka, vestiges of hemp were discovered (Hansson and Dickson 1997, 209). Written sources from the Middle Ages state that the production of hemp was important, for instance, for the manufacture of coarse hangings and rope. The nettle is another plant that has been used for fibre. Nettle fibres are finer and shorter than flax and are less durable. To make the hemp and nettle fibres spinnable, they are prepared in the same way as flax.

Other fibres, which could be used, come from the bast of lime, willow and poplar. There are several finds of silk textiles in Viking Age Birka, but both yarn and cloth must have been imported (Geijer 1994, 134).

Metal thread

Metal thread has also been used for the production of certain textiles, above all the tablet-woven bands and *passementerie* (see below). In the manufacture of metal thread, a special wire-drawing instrument was used; one of these has been found in the Black Earth at Birka (Arrhenius 1968, 288–293). In this case the starting material was a 3–4 mm thick wire of gold or silver, and the finished product was 0.1–0.5 mm thick. This 'drawn thread' is solid, with a round cross-section. This type of thread was the most common metal thread in Birka.

Another type of metal thread was *lamella*, a thin strip of metal which has been rolled or hammered from a wire or a small strip of gold foil, silver foil, or other metal (Strömberg *et al.* 1979, 15, 48). The *lamella* can be spun round a core of organic material, such as silk but only a few of the tablet woven bands from Birka were made with this type of thread.

DYEING

The analysis of archaeological textile material shows, that people in the Viking Age dyed textiles. Not only were garments entirely or partly dyed, but also other textiles, such as hangings, were made of yarn dyed in different colours and shades (Franzén and Nockert 1992, 20). However, it is difficult to determine how common this practice was, since the colour of textiles has either not been preserved or has changed while in the soil. Numerous plants give a lasting colour, and there may have been widespread knowledge about their use. Analyses of dyed textiles have shown that blue was obtained from woad, while red could be produced with madder or plants such as hedge bedstraw or northern bedstraw. Yellow colours could be obtained from plants like weld (Dyer's Rocket) and alpine bearberry.

Wool is simpler to dye than flax since the dye adheres better to wool fibres than to flax fibres. Furthermore, different sheep have various shades of brown and grey, and there can even be several natural shades in the fleece of the animal. These various natural colours were also utilized in textile manufacture. Sometimes these different colours were sorted and spun separately, taking advantage of the shades in the weave. Flax fibres could be bleached by various methods.

TEXTILE TOOLS AND TOOL MANUFACTURE

Iron Age people knew and used several types of textile tools for different techniques. Several of the tools used during the Viking Age remained in use well into historic times, and there is sufficient knowledge about how they were employed. Even if the textile tools that have developed in more recent times, such as the spinning wheel and the treadle loom, are more efficient and make it possible to produce more complex textiles, we should not underestimate the Viking Age implements and above all the different ways in which they were used. Just because the tools look simple, it does not mean that what was made using them was simple or coarse. Thus, complex tablet-woven bands can be produced with the aid of simple tablets of wood or leather. Even though the tools are simple, the bands can in some cases withstand comparison with modern applied textile art.

Another example is the fabric known as 2/1 twill, which most scholars assumed was impossible to weave on a warp-weighted loom (*e.g.* Hoffmann 1964). Finds of textiles in this weave were even cited as evidence for the use of treadle looms. Experiments carried out at Lejre Experimental Centre in Denmark in the 1980s and 1990s demonstrated clearly that it was no more difficult to weave a 2/1 twill than a 2/2 twill on a warp-weighted loom (Andersson 2000, 174).

The following account of the different tools and techniques is a broad survey of the textile techniques used and the function and potential of the tools.

SPINNING TOOLS

The most frequently found spinning tool from the Viking Age is the spindle. A spindle consists of a rod and a whorl (Fig. 6.3). There are no finds of spindle rods from Birka. However, since wooden rods have been found on other Viking Age settlements, we can assume that the rods used in Birka too had been made of wood.

The spindle whorls uncovered in archaeological excavations vary in regard to material, shape and size. They were usually made of stones such as sandstone, fired clay or bone, but whorls of other, more exotic materials, such as glass and amber, have also been found. At Birka, there are many archaeological finds of spindle whorls made in different shapes and sizes.

The spindle whorl can be placed at different heights on the spindle. The whorl is usually placed on the lower part of the rod, giving a low whorl spindle, or on the upper part, giving a high whorl spindle. The placing of the whorl affects how the spindle is rotated. If the whorl is at the bottom, the whorl is activated by twisting the upper part of the stick. If the whorl is at the top, the spindle can be rotated either by moving it against the thigh or by twisting the lower part of the spindle. In archaeological digs it is rare to find a whole spindle with the whorl still attached to the rod. It is nevertheless likely that both low whorl and high whorl spindles were used in Scandinavia during the Viking Age.

After the preparation of the rolag, the wool is twisted by hand into a short thread which is attached to the rod. The spindle can then hang freely. Thereafter the rod is rotated while the spinner simultaneously draws out the fibres, and it is the twisting of the fibres around their own axis that forms the thread. When a certain length has been spun, the thread is wound up on the spindle and it is then possible to continue spinning. The process is repeated until the spindle rod is filled with thread.

When the rod is full, the spun yarn is wound onto a reel or niddy noddy (Fig. 6.4). None have been found in Birka but they are known from other places, for instance, the Oseberg grave in Norway (Hoffmann 1991, 164). When the yarn is removed from the spindle rod it is 'alive' and can easily get tangled, which can cause problems when setting up the warp threads on a loom. A solution to this problem is to let the thread stay stretched on a reel for a while.

The parameters that affect the quality of the spun thread are the fibre material and the weight and diameter of the whorl. Experiments have demonstrated that a very thin thread can be spun with a light small spindle whorl, and a much coarser thread with a spindle whorl that is heavy and large (Holm 1996; Andersson 1999, 2003).

The quality of the wool affects above all the manufacture of the finer threads. Experiments have shown that with very light whorls weighing under 10 g one can spin

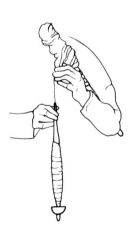

Fig. 6.3: Low-whorl spindle with rod and whorl. A distaff is used when spinning. (©Eva B. Andersson)

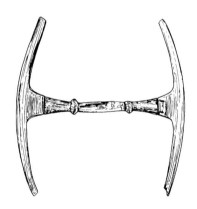

Fig. 6.4: Reel, width approx. 30 cm. (After Grieg 1928)

yarn of a very fine quality, comparable to the Viking Age yarns found in the Birka burials. The same spindle cannot be used to spin a coarser thread. It was also demonstrated that rods of less than 15 cm in length could have been used as spindles; when spinning with a very light whorl, a shorter rod is necessary to achieve balance in the spindle (Andersson 1999, 2003).

The study of the spindle whorls from Birka showed that the whorl weight varied from 2 g to 134 g, but weights between 5 g and 40 g were the most common. Altogether the result indicates that the yarn produced at Birka included both finely spun thread for luxury fabrics, and coarser yarn, for instance for sailcloth (Andersson 2003, 73).

LOOMS AND WEAVING

Cloth is a result of weaving two thread systems crossing each other at right angles. One of these systems, the warp, is kept stretched during the weaving. The other thread system, the weft, runs alternately over and under the warp threads. The warp must be strong if it is to hold when the threads are stretched, so it is often more tightly spun than the weft. The appearance of the fabric depends on (1) the weaving technique that is used, (2) whether the yarn is fine or coarse and (3) whether the thread is tightly or loosely spun.

The thread count shows the number of warp and weft threads per cm. A well-balanced fabric has an equal number of warp and weft threads.

The system in which the warp and weft are interwoven to make a fabric is called the weave or binding. It is always the warp that binds the weft. To achieve a weave, some warp threads must be raised or lowered between each new pick. This action in weaving is called changing the shed (a space between the warp threads into which the weft can be inserted). By varying how many warp threads are raised or lowered between the picks, different weaves can be obtained. The basic weaving techniques are tabby, twill, and satin. Twill weave can be varied by alternating the binding points in several different variants, for example, 2/2 twill, 2/1 twill, diamond twill, and chevron twill (Fig. 6.5). To weave a non-continuous pattern, for example, a tapestry, one uses weaving techniques such as brocade (*e.g.* soumak and brocaded tabby) and tapestry weave (see *e.g.* Strömberg *et al.* 1979; Franzén and Nockert 1992, 15; Geijer 1994, 58).

The warp-weighted loom

Weaving is accomplished on a loom. The loom that has left its traces in the Scandinavian Viking Age archaeological record is the warp-weighted loom (Fig. 6.6). This loom is upright and the warp is kept stretched by loom weights. Loom weights are the main archaeological evidence for this type of loom. The weights found in Birka were made of clay, as was common during the Viking Age in this region. The weights vary in size and shape. Generally speaking, lighter weights are suitable for fabrics with thin warp threads, while heavier weights are more useful for fabrics with thick warp threads.

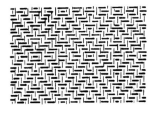 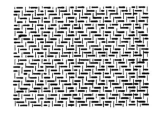

Fig. 6.5: Different types of weave. Top left: diamond (goose eye) twill. Top right: broken lozenge twill. Centre left: 2/2 twill. Centre right: chevron twill; bottom left tabby. Bottom right: 2/1 twill. (©Eva B. Andersson)

The analysis of the loom weights from Birka shows that loom weights of different sizes had been used. The loom weights vary from 200 g to 1900 g in weight, but the results of the study indicate that weights between 400 g and 800 g were the most common (Andersson 2003, 80).

The width and length of the warp is determined above all by the dimensions one wants the finished fabric to have, although, of course, the size of the loom limits the width. Still, data from Iceland show that a piece of cloth woven on a warp-weighted loom could be as much as 12.5 m long (Geijer 1965, 118).

When weaving on a warp-weighted loom one stands in front of it and weaves from the top downwards. The weft is inserted between the warp threads and beaten upwards with the aid of a sword beater. There are no finds of

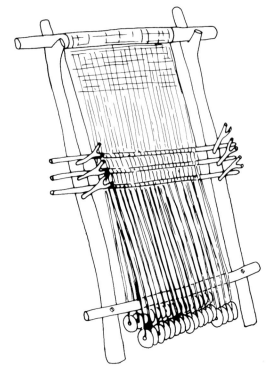

Fig. 6.6: Warp-weighted loom (height approx. 1.7 m). (©Eva B. Andersson)

sword beaters from Birka, but other finds from Viking Age graves suggest that the beaters were made of wood, bone and/or iron. (Hoffmann 1991, 176).

The two-beam loom (Fig. 6.7)

Another type of loom used in prehistoric times was the two-beam vertical loom, but there are few archaeological traces of this since it was made entirely of wood. Like the warp-weighted loom, the two-beam loom stands upright. The length of the warp is somewhat limited to the height of the loom, since the warp threads are stretched by being attached to the loom. If a longer piece of cloth is needed, the warp-weighted loom is thus preferable.

It is difficult to see from the surviving textile fragments whether they were woven on a two-beam loom or a warp-weighted loom (Hald 1980, 210). Today, the vertical two-beam loom is still used in certain parts of Norway for weaving coarser pattern-woven textiles, such as bedspreads. Different types of combs are used to beat the weft in the different patterns (Hoffmann 1991, 178).

In Birka a couple of weaving combs have been found, but coarse bone needles may have been used for pattern weaving with the simultaneous use of several weft threads, mostly of different colours. To keep track of these threads and to make it easier to insert the picks, the weft is threaded onto a bigger needle.

OTHER TECHNIQUES AND TOOLS

Tablet weaving (Fig. 6.8)

Bands woven with the aid of thin, squared tablets with holes for the warp are called tablet-woven. The finished result can vary from simple bands woven with four tablets to exclusive bands with silk and metal threads pattern-woven with more than 150 tablets (Hald 1980, 229). The simpler bands were used, among other things, to edge cloths, while the exclusive pattern-woven bands served as costume decoration. Tablets have been found, for instance, at Birka but also at Oseberg in Norway (Grieg 1928; Geijer 1938).

A simple way to make tablet woven bands is to hang the warp from a hook in the ceiling and stretch it with loom weights. Another way, the one most frequently used today, is to stretch the warp horizontally by tying one end of the warp to a hook and attaching the other end to a belt worn round the waist; instead of weights, the warp is stretched by the weaver's own body. To weave the simplest type of band, one then turns all the tablets a quarter-turn to create a shed. The tablets are then turned yet another quarter-turn, and hence the threads too. A new weft thread is then inserted in the new shed that is formed, and so the process continues. In pattern weaving, each tablet can be turned individually.

Tablet bands have been found in about 60 Birka graves. Many of them are woven with gold or silver threads as weft (Geijer 1938; Hägg 1986, 52).

Fig. 6.8: Tablets for tablet weaving, tablets measuring approx. 3.5 by 3.5 cm. (©Eva B. Andersson)

Fig. 6.7: Two beam loom with tapestry (height 1.1 m, width 66–67 cm). (After the Oseberg find)

Passementerie and other techniques

Textiles made with the techniques of plaiting, sprang, and *passementerie* have also been found in Birka (Geijer 1938, 99; Hald 1980, 240; Hägg 1983, 208; 1986, 52). Special tools are not usually necessary for plaiting. Among the plaits used for bands and straps are diagonal plaits. Sprang is a technique used for hoods and the like. The work may have been done on a simple wooden frame with the aid of thin sticks or perhaps bones. *Passementerie* is an umbrella term for decorative trimmings (borders, fringes, tassels, and the like) made of gold or silver thread, different colours of yarn, and other materials. Many techniques included here, such as twisting, braiding, lacemaking, band weaving, and embroidery often occur simultaneously (Geijer 1938, 99).

A large number of *passementerie* items of gold and silver thread such as various types of embroideries and brocading have been found in the Birka graves (Geijer 1938). All these textiles are very well made, indicating high professional skill. Several of these *passementerie* items are probably closely related to *macramé*, a complex plaiting technique (de Dillmont 1987, 413). Apart from a device for holding the loose vertical threads, few or no tools are needed. If one works with many long threads, however, it can be an advantage to have the threads rolled up on a bobbin or the like.

FINISHING AND DECORATION OF TEXTILES

Fulling

Fulling is a process involving the preparation of woollen fabric with water and sometimes soap. The result is a very tight fabric. The method has been used, for example, in the manufacture of outer garments and sailcloth. If a fabric is to be fulled, it is important that at least the weft is made of wool.

Needles and single-needle knitting

Textile work requires many needles of different sizes. Analyses of textiles have shown that Viking Age people used several of the sewing techniques that are still used today (Hald 1980, 281). For sewing thin fabrics, fine needles, often made of metal, were used. Thin metal needles, like the sewing needles used today, were also employed for needlework and embroidery. Examples of various embroidery techniques found in the Birka textiles are stem stitch and chain stitch (Geijer 1938, 108). In Birka, there are several archaeological finds of thin, metal needles and many finds of needle boxes. It is interesting to note that the needle boxes found in the graves are usually made of metal such as bronze, while the needle boxes found at the settlement area were made of bone (Andersson 2003).

The needles more commonly found in Birka are made of bone (Andersson 2003). Bone needles may have been used for single-needle knitting, a technique which can be used to make socks and mittens, but no coarse textiles made with this technique have been preserved from the Viking Age. However, there are several medieval finds of textiles made by single-needle knitting (Hald 1980, 299, 302).

Coarse, bone needles may, as mentioned before, have been used for pattern weaving. Big needles may also have been used as shuttles by winding the weft onto the needle and inserting it through the shed. The needles used for these operations did not need to be sharp-pointed since they were not meant to perforate the cloth.

Coarse, pointed bone needles on the other hand may be suitable for sewing or darning thick woollen fabric. It is also likely that people used a bone needle or awl to make holes in very thick, fulled fabrics before sewing.

Other textile tools and techniques

Pleating is a technique that is often mentioned in connection with linen fabrics, but woollen material can also be pleated. Pleating is done by sewing small folds, 2–3 mm deep, with needle and thread. The threads are then pulled so that the cloth is wrinkled, after which it is moistened and put in a press until the folds are made permanent. The threads are then removed from the cloth. This technique forms low, round standing folds. The term pleating also includes pressing a pattern into fabric, so the technique described above is commonly called *plissé* or in Swedish *rynkveckning* to avoid confusion (Geijer 1980, 214). There are several examples of the use of this technique in the linen textile finds in Birka (Hägg 1974).

TEXTILE PRODUCTION AND ITS IMPACT ON SOCIETY

The textile tools, especially spindle whorls, show that textile production in Birka was extensive and varied. Research has demonstrated that the inhabitants of Birka had all the necessary tools for making the range of qualities of wool and linen cloth found in the graves. Moreover, the tools demonstrate that everything from finer to coarser textiles was produced (Andersson 2003, 99). This clearly contradicts the previous assumption that indigenous textile production in Birka comprised only coarse woollen cloth of poor quality (*e.g.* Geijer 1938; 1965; Hoffmann 1964; Hägg 1974).

While the loom weights are far too fragmentary to allow any assessment, the spindle whorls, the sewing needles, and the bone needle boxes seem standardized in shape. Spindle whorls of stone were either made in Birka out of imported raw material or were brought to the site ready-made. Some of the tools were probably made by a specialized craftsman and not by the user (Andersson 2003, 148).

Textile tools have been found all over the excavated area, and there is no evidence of specific production at any particular place in the excavated part of the settlement. However, it should be kept in mind that only 6–7% of the settlement area has so far been investigated.

The number of finds of textile tools increases during the 10th century AD. Whether this reflects an actual increase in production is impossible to establish, since there are several aspects to take into consideration. Still, much suggests that the settlement expanded during this period, meaning that more textiles must have been produced to satisfy household requirements. Another factor is that it is difficult today to determine whether equally large areas have been excavated from the 8th, 9th, and 10th centuries AD. The evaluation of the tools likewise does not show that there was any specific type of textile manufacture in any period or that the production changed during the lifetime of Birka.

There are, with some exceptions, few finds of textile tools from the graves. They only occur in about 153 graves. In addition, the finds represent types of textile tools – metal needle boxes, smoothing stones, and scissors – which are not very frequent in the settlement. I do not believe that the tools found in the graves represent specialist textile workers. According to Icelandic sources, wealthy women did not weave cloth for everyday use: they sewed and sometimes spun (Porláksson 1981, 61). In the graves, there are no finds of loom weights, just a few spindle whorls, and several finds of needle cases and scissors which support this interpretation. The weavers and those who spun most of the thread and combed the wool are so far invisible and the question is: can they and their work ever become visible?

By studying the textile tools, we get a picture of the textiles manufactured at Birka, a picture different from the one suggested by merely studying the textiles themselves. There were many people living in Birka, men, women and children, people with different backgrounds and status. All of them needed clothing and other types of textile. No wonder that so many textile tools have been found.

Textile manufacture just for everyday use must have taken up a great deal of time. Just to produce two costumes, one female and one male, a spinner needed to spin approximately 42,600 m of yarn (Andersson 2003, 47). The knowledge and skill to produce textiles must have been lodged in more than one person. Several people were involved in the production process which included the harvesting of fibres, preparing them for spinning, weaving, various finishing processes and finally sewing them into clothing and other products. Could these textiles have been produced in every household at Birka? I would define the Birka house-hold production of textiles in the following way:

–   the production solely covered the household's own needs;
–   household members possessed general knowledge and skills;
–   raw materials were commonly accessible;
–   textile manufacture was not a full time occupation.

Many of the textiles for everyday use could have been produced in this mode, especially by ordinary people; but there is the question of where they got the raw material from. It is quite likely that at least some of it was imported. In order to produce costumes for 300 people, at least 900 kg of raw material would have been needed.

Even if most of the textiles were produced in a household context, another possibility is that spinners and weavers manufactured textiles in their homes in household industry mode or in a putting out mode. This kind of production can be defined as follows:

–   the production scale was beyond the needs of the producers;
–   it was organised at household level;
–   the members of the household possessed general knowledge and skills;
–   there was a surplus of raw material and/or the buyers provided them with raw material;
–   they did not work full time.

Could some of the sophisticated textiles, despite earlier suggestions, have been manufactured at Birka and, in that case, in what organisational mode? On the basis of the results of the Birka corpus of tools, I believe that at least some of these fine quality textiles were manufactured here, although not in every single household. Neither do I believe that these textiles were manufactured in workshops since there is no archaeological evidence for the latter (yet). The mode I think most credible is an 'attached specialist production'. For this mode I suggest that:

–   high quality products were made;
–   production was by craft specialists and their skills were enhanced by full-time occupation;
–   craftspeople were supported by and dependent on patrons;
–   they worked on a full- time basis;
–   the raw materials were of a better and/or higher quality.

To produce such textiles a great deal of time and skills are needed. The wool could have been imported as raw material from some foreign countries, and also some of the textile craftspeople could have come from abroad. Much of the raw material for different types of crafts, as well as the knowledge and skills to work them, were imported to Birka. It is quite possible that some of the chieftains and/or the rich merchants brought both raw material and even a textile worker or two home from a journey. It is also possible that these specialists in turn taught their techniques to some of the local inhabitants.

I believe that these specialists produced only for their patron, and that the textiles they produced could be given as gifts. It is, of course, also quite possible that the chieftains could support these craftspeople in order to manufacture textiles for their patrons and their families' everyday use.

There is one more group of possible textile workers that should be mentioned, namely, high-ranking women. When women of high status are mentioned in Norse sagas in connection with textile manufacturing, it seems that they are not producing 'every day' textiles but rather more exclusive textiles like tapestries and embroideries. It is consequently possible that elite women in Birka produced sophisticated textiles as the tools from the graves partly suggest.

CONCLUSIONS

This chapter demonstrates how useful it is to combine knowledge of textiles and textile production to gain a better picture of the impact of textile production on society. The textiles and the traces of textile production give us the opportunity to interpret and discuss textile craft in Viking Age Birka. My investigation shows that production at Birka has been more complex and specialised than hitherto thought. It was organized most likely in different modes and both specialists and non-specialists may have been involved in the manufacturing process. There is clear evidence of specialist crafts at Birka, and it is not surprising that some of the textiles also could have been produced by specialists. Some of the raw material has been imported from the Mälar region, but it could also come from more distant places.

The textiles give us one picture and the tools another; by comparing and combining them and the contexts in which they are found we are able to show the importance of textile work in the Viking Age. The high status costumes give us information about the complex techniques and skilled craftsmanship involved in the production of luxury items. The tools, on the other hand, give us a picture of the textiles people needed for every day use and the textiles that were produced locally. At the same time, the tools show us that there existed a highly specialised textile production in Birka in contrast to the situation in the agrarian settlements in the Mälar Region. We know that exclusive textiles often were given as gifts and commanded a high value. We know that sails must have been as valuable as the ship. We know that everybody needed textiles. The investigation of the textiles and the textile tools found in Birka elucidates supports and confirms this.

ACKNOWLEDGEMENTS

I would like to thank Tina Borstam and Annika Jeppsson who produced my illustrations. Parts of this chapter have previously been published in Andersson 2003 and 2007.

BIBLIOGRAPHY

Adalsteinsson, S. (1990) Importance of sheep in early Icelandic agriculture. In G. F. Biglow (ed.) *The Norse of the North Atlantic,* Acta Archaeologica 61. Copenhagen, 285–291.

Ambrosiani, B. (1985) Specialization and urbanization in the Mälaren Valley – a question of maturity. In Sven Olaf Lindquist (ed.) *Society and Trade in the Baltic during the Viking Age*, Acta Visbyensia VII. Visby, 103–112.

Ambrosiani, B. and H. Clark (1991) *Towns in the Viking Age.* Leicester, Leicester University Press.

Ambrosiani, B. and B. G. Erikson (1996) *Birka vikingastaden* 5. Sveriges Radios förlag.

Andersson, E. (1999) *The Common Thread. Textile Production during the Late Iron Age – Viking Age.* Institute of Archaeology, Report Series 67. Lund.

Andersson, E. (2000) Textilproduktion i Löddeköpinge – endast för husbehov? In F. Svanberg and B. Söderberg (eds) *Porten till Skåne, Löddeköpinge under järnålder och medeltid.* Riksantikvarieämbetet, Arkeologiska undersökningar, Skrifter 3, 158–187.

Andersson, E. (2003) *Tools for Textile Production from Birka and Hedeby.* Birka Studies 8. Stockholm.

Andersson, E. B. (2007) Engendering Central Places, some aspects of the organisation of textile production during the Viking Age. In A. Rast-Eicher and R. Windler (eds) *NESAT IX Archäologische Textilfunde – Archaeological Textiles.* Ennenda, ArcheoTex, 148–153.

Arbman, H. (1955) *Svear i Österviking.* Stockholm.

Arrhenius, B. (1968) Prehistoric Scandinavian Textiles. *Fornvännen* 63, 288–293.

Bender Jørgensen, L. (1986) *Forhistoriske tekstiler i Skandinavien.* Nordiske Fortidsminder serie B: 9. Copenhagen, Kongelige Nordiske Oldskriftselskab.

de Dillmont, T. (1987) *Encyclopedia of Needlework.* New York, Crescent.

Franzén, A.-M. and M. Nockert (1992) *Bonaderna från Skog och Överhogdal och andra medeltida väggbeklädnader.* Stockholm, Kungl. Vitterhets Historie och Antikvitets Akademien.

Geijer, A. (1938) *Die Textilfunde aus den Gräbern.* Birka III. Stockholm, Kungliga Vitterhets-, Historie- och Antikvitets Akademien.

Geijer, A. (1965) Var järnålderns 'frisiska kläde' tillverkat i Syrien? Reflektioner i anslutning till ett arbete om tyngdvävstolen, *Fornvännen* 60, 112–132.

Geijer, A. (1980) The textile finds from Birka. *Acta Archaeologica* 50, 209–222.

Geijer, A. (1994) *Ur textilkonstens historia.* Stockholm, Tiden.

Gräslund, A.-S. (1980) *The Burial Custom, A Study of the Graves on Björkö.* Birka IV. Stockholm, Kungliga Vitterhets-, Historie- och Antikvitets Akademien.

Grieg, S. (1928) Kongsgaarden. In A.W. Brøgger and H. Schetelig (eds) *Osebergfundet* 2. Kristiania, Universitets Oldsaksamling.

Hägg, I. (1974) *Kvinnodräkten i Birka.* Report Series: AUN 2. Uppsala, Institute of North European Archaeology, Uppsala University.

Hägg, I. (1983) Birkas orientaliska praktplagg. *Fornvännen* 78, 259–278.

Hägg, I. (1986) Die Tracht. *Birka* II:2. Kungl. Vitterhets Historie och Antikvitets Akademien, 51–72.

Hägg, I. (1987) Textilhistoria, statistik och källkritik. *Tor*, 21, 283–296.

Hald, M. (1980) *Ancient Danish textiles from bogs and burials, a comparative study of costumes and Iron Age textiles.* Copenhagen, National Museum of Denmark.

Hansson, A.-M. and J. H. Dickson (1997) Plant Remains in Sediment from the Björkö Strait Outside the Black Earth at the Viking Age Town of Birka, Eastern Central Sweden. In U. Miller *et al.* (eds) *Environment and Vikings with Special Reference to Birka.* PACT 52 = Birka Studies 4. Rixensart and Stockholm, 205–216.

Hoffmann, M. (1964) *The warp-weighted loom.* Oslo, Universitetsforlaget.

Hoffmann, M. (1991) *Fra fiber til tøy.* Oslo, Landbruksforlaget.

Holm, C. (1996) Experiment med sländspinning. In E. Andersson *Textilproduktion i arkeologisk konetxt, en metodstudie av yngre järnåldersboplatser i Skåne.* University of Lund, Institute of Archaeology Report Series No. 58, 111–116. Lund.

Ingstad, A. S. (1980) 'Frisisk klede'? En diskusjon omkring noen fine tekstiler fra yngre jernalder. *Viking*, 43, 81–95.

Ingstad, A. S. (2006) Brukstekstilene. In A.-E. Christensen and M. Nockert (eds) *Osebergfunnet. Bind IV. Tekstilene.* Oslo, 185–275. Nockert, M. and L. R. Knudsen (1996) Gotländska brickband från vikingatiden. *Gotländskt Arkiv*, 68, 41–46. Visby.

Pedersen, E. A., M. Widgren and S. Welinder (1998) *Jordbrukets första femtusen år, 4000 f. Kr. – 1000 e. Kr.* Stockholm, Natur och kultur.

Porláksson, H. (1981) Arbeidskvinnens, särlig veverskans økonomiske stilling på island i middelalderen. In H. Gunneng and B. Strand (eds) *Kvinnans ekonomiska ställning under nordisk medeltid.* Göteborg, 1–65.

Strömberg, E., Geijer, A., Hald, M. and Hoffman, M., 1979 (1967). *Nordisk textilteknisk terminologi.* Oslo.

Szabó, Mátyás (1970) *Herdar och husdjur.* Nordiska Museets Handlingar. Lund.

Chapter 7

Spotlight on Medieval Scandinavian Dress: Sources and Interpretations

Kathrine Vestergaard Pedersen

In contrast to many other historical eras, the Medieval Period has a great number of sources of information on contemporary dress and clothing: preserved and complete archaeological garments, visual artefacts such as murals and sepulchral monuments and written evidence such as wills and laws. Although the source material seems extensive in comparison to other periods, there are still many interpretational problems and 'black holes' that make the reconstruction of medieval dress problematic. This chapter presents the different types of sources and gives examples of how the sources can be used in reconstructing a garment.

Keywords: medieval, Greenland, reconstruction, Lödöse, craft, weaving.

RECONSTRUCTING MEDIEVAL TAILORING TODAY

Making a medieval costume today can be a treasure hunt through pictures, documents and archaeological finds. There is an abundance of source material to make reconstructions from: images of medieval garments, as well as details of fabrics, colours, patterns and sewing techniques and information on dress from different social, political and economic contexts. However, this rich material can also create problems, when the right sources for the right time, place and person have to be found.

The first step in tailoring a medieval garment is to consider its purpose. Is it merely to give an illusion as through a camera lens, as in a theatrical costume, or is it a dress that has to be worn and used, so fabric qualities and sewing techniques may be studied and a physical impression of how medieval clothing feels like may be obtained? The latter can be called a reconstruction. A reconstruction of medieval clothing can be done from different perspectives. We can choose a picture, a written description or an archaeological find and try to recreate that, or we can choose a character, a person of certain social status and investigate what kind of dress this person would wear. In both cases, there will be some black holes, which we have to fill by putting together different sources to form the basis of a complete costume. Either way, we have to establish time, place and social context for our reconstruction before starting the search for documentation and sources.

The second step is to consider what elements a garment consists of. The basic elements are of course a fabric, a pattern and seams. Each of these three elements can vary and have different looks and details. However, clothing can also consist of several garments and accessories such as undergarments, overgarments, shoes, laces and headgear.

The way I reconstruct medieval clothing is through a study of pattern and cut and a number of archaeological finds. I have tried to make medieval clothing based on the source material and with each attempt, my knowledge and ability has grown and the garments developed from mere images of medieval clothes into actual reconstructions (Vestergaard Pedersen 2004b).

THE SOURCES

Written documents are an excellent source of information about what people of different social, political and economical levels wore in Medieval times. Names of different fabrics, garment types and colours are mentioned in wills, inventories or laws. These documents can give us information about how medieval people thought of fabrics and clothing: what ideals they had for clothing and what they thought was important about colours, fabrics, patterns and decorations (Dahl 2005, 25–28). However, the written sources do not give any detailed descriptions of patterns, sewing techniques or fabric qualities. To find this information we need to study archaeological finds – the physical evidence of medieval dress.

The archaeological evidence consists of a series of complete garments found together with bodies in bogs and burial sites and a large number of fragments found in deposits and pits in medieval towns (Nørlund 1924; Hald 1980; Maik 1998; Crowfoot *et al.* 2001; Østergård 2004). The archaeological evidence also includes tools for tailoring and textile production that indirectly can provide information about fabric qualities and production methods (see Andersson in this volume). From the archaeological material, it is possible to find evidence of patterns – how for instance the garments were shaped and cut, the pieces sewn together, the types of stitches and sewing threads used and how the garments were decorated. It is also possible to find traces of colours and dyeing materials and techniques, as well as fabric quality; the various raw materials; how the threads are spun and the fabric woven and treated afterwards. Yet, it must be remembered that the archaeological evidence provides only traces of the past. We can look at the material and describe what we see, but because there are no written notes on the objects, we cannot answer questions such as by or for whom, when or how the object was made (Vedeler 2004, 57–59). We can never understand the archaeological finds completely, albeit we can come closer to an interpretation by comparing them with either written sources or pictures.

Pictures give us information of the visual impression of fabrics and clothing. How the clothes were worn and draped on the body, how men, women and children were dressed and how fashion changed and developed overall. To identify dress and single types of garments in pictures can, however, be a complex matter (see Engelhardt Mathiassen and Leilund in this volume). There are no words and terms on the pictures that can link an actual look to a single garment type, and details such as seams are rarely available. Often the pictures are used to tell a story or send a message and the clothing can have been used more as a symbol of social or economic status than a realistic illustration of what people actually wore (Bolvig 2003). Several specific examples of sources follow.

Medieval costume from a Scandinavian settlement in Greenland

In 1921, when the churchyard at Herjolfsnes (Ikigaat, south-west Greenland) was excavated, several graves were found where the deceased had been placed in either coffins or shrouds. The shrouds were made of everyday garments worn by the Norse people and cut up for use as burial cloths. Several tunics, hoods, stockings, hats, caps and children's garments were found. All were made of a special type of wool fabric that has only been found in Greenland. Many details, such as decorations and seams, were also preserved. All the tunics had different patterns because each garment had been sewn individually; however, it is possible to group them into types according to number and appearance of gores. Many of the garments are radiocarbon-dated from the end of the 13th century to the 15th century. Although many pattern and sewing details can be studied, and their context as everyday garments with secondary use as shrouds is relatively certain, the special fabric known only from Greenland suggests that the information in the find can't be applied to all of Scandinavia or Northern Europe. Furthermore, due to the character of the shrouds, we cannot say anything about the combinations of garments and whole costumes (Nørlund 1924; Østergård 2004).

The patterns of a small number of the garments have been copied and made available at the National Museum of Denmark's gift shop in Copenhagen. One of these, number 39, can be described as a short-sleeved garment in a reddish-brown colour (Fig. 7.1). It consists of a front and back piece with central gores in the front and back and gores in each side. The side gores are narrow at the upper end and build the armhole together with front and back pieces. The sleeves are short with a triangular gore at the back of the shoulder blade to give space for movement. The central gores are placed relatively high. The front piece is longer than the back piece, and the garment is slightly uneven. The neck opening is also relatively wide with a small slit in front. Furthermore, a number of different seams and details can be studied, for example the warp has originally been dyed but the weft left undyed (Østergård 2004).

There is very little information about the person who was buried in the dress. In contrast to the textiles, the skeletons were very poorly preserved. The only information that this skeleton provided is that it was a woman. The fact that the clothing had been cut up and used as a shroud also indicates that dress and buried person perhaps did not match

Fig. 7.1: Garment no. 39 from Herjolfsnes, Greenland. (National Museum of Denmark, Nr D10581)

in life. As far as the pattern is concerned, the principle with straight up and down front and back pieces adjusted in width with gores is known from other finds for example Bocksten in Southwest Sweden, Skjoldehamn in Northern Norway, Moselund and Kragelund in Denmark (Gjessing 1938; Nockert 1997; Østergård 2004). Only Bocksten has been dated to the same period as Herjolfsnes, the rest are older, but none of these finds have exactly the same cut of side gores, armholes or sleeves. The closest parallels to the triangular gusset in the sleeve appear on the golden gown of Queen Margrete I, (1353–1412) the joint regent of Denmark, Norway and Sweden, and the *pourpoint of* Charles de Blois, Duke of Brittany (1319–1364) (Geijer *et al.* 1994, 48, 72–74). However, both of these garments have several gussets and are more sophisticated in make.

Medieval costume in murals

Murals from Højby Church in Zealand, Denmark, relate a legend of a young man making advances to a young woman, but as the woman rejects him, he accuses her of theft and she gets her hand cut off. However, St. James makes it whole again. The mural is dated to the 1380s (Saxtorph 1997, 96–97) (Figs 7.2–7.3). The woman's dress is a type of long tunic with long sleeves and a floor-length, wide skirt. The dress is relatively close-fitting. In the first scene, it looks as if the dress either has a belt or is divided at the waist; in the second scene, there is no evidence of belt or waistline, but the bodice is closed in the front with a lace. There are green cuffs at the wrists. The neck opening is relatively wide with a square cut. The woman's head is covered with a white veil. The colour of the dress seems to be reddish.

The mural has been interpreted as a legend known from written sources. We do not know if there was a symbolic reason as to why the woman has a close fitted dress or the kind of headdress she wears or its social status. Perhaps the colours of the dress are also significant, but it is possible the artist merely found that the colours looked good together. It is also possible that her appearance and dress simply are in accordance with the stereotype of young women in this period. If so, we learn that the dresses were floor-length, with close-fitted laced bodices widening out at the hips. However, no information about pattern, sewing techniques or fabrics can be obtained from the mural.

Medieval costume in written sources

An example of the information that can be gathered from written documents is a list of items, such as tunics, cloaks, headgear and ornaments that a woman brought with her into a marriage (Dahl forthcoming). Among the items mentioned are a red tunic (*kiurtil*) with hood (*kapprun*), a blue tunic, another red tunic and a red marbled one (*mængiadhr*), hoods with ermine, miniver and silk lining, a marbled mantle (*mattul*) with miniver, another hood with ermine and a fur cap of miniver. In addition there are: a blue marbled tunic, some decoration edgings or borders (*lodh*), a red marbled mantle with miniver and decoration (*safal*), a marbled supertunic (*syrkot*), several head coverings or veils (*hauudh dukar* and *skaut*) and some metal ornaments such as belts and brooches (Fig. 7.4).

All items of clothing are valued in monetary terms, but to know their true contemporary value they have to be compared with a great deal of other inventories and wills. However, it is clear how little information the written documents actually give for reconstruction purposes. Different garment types are listed such as tunics (*kiurtil*), hoods (*kapprun*) and cloaks (*mattul*) and the colours are often also stated as red, blue or marbled. In addition, decoration, jewellery and fur are mentioned, but never any information about the shape or look of the clothing.

An impression of the standards and ideals of the time may be found in an extract of Saint Bridget of Sweden's revelation in 1378–79 (Dahl forthcoming) (Fig. 7.5). Here she claims that the reason for the outbreak of the plague in *ca.* 1350 is the way people were dressed. She calls for humility in dress: neither too long, nor too short nor tight, nor too

Fig. 7.2: Church mural of the legend of St. James, Højby Church, Denmark, 1380s. (Courtesy of Camilla Luise Dahl; Photo: Jens Christian Lund)

ostentatious in cut and pattern. She emphasizes that bodices have to be modest and not pretentious with lacing, buttons or knots. Women should not wear exposing or accentuating clothing because it is the Devil's work when women dress unsuitably, thereby provoking lust and insulting God.

*Fig. 7.3: Church mural of the legend of St. James, Højby Church, Denmark, 1380s. (Courtesy of
Camilla Luise Dahl; Photo: Jens Christian Lund)*

These are merely three examples of different sources on medieval clothing and dress. If
we were to put the three types of sources together, it is obvious that we could obtain a
clearer picture. Each type of source has first to be thoroughly studied and interpreted,
before they can be linked together and used to provide information about dress and
clothing. The mural perhaps makes more sense when it is interpreted and understood in
the light of Saint Bridget's revelation. Comparing sources from different contexts, places
and times can, however, be a difficult process.

AN EXAMPLE OF A RECONSTRUCTION OF A MEDIEVAL DRESS

Four years ago, I made a medieval dress for myself. After a few attempts with bought
fabrics and the pattern from Herjolfsnes, I decided to weave the fabric. I used the
publications of Poul Nørlund and Else Østergård which recommended the use of single
spun threads in wool with a darker colour in warp and lighter colour in weft (Nørlund
1924; Østergård 1987). This was my first weaving project and I received the help of a
highly skilled modern hand weaver. I obtained single spun wool yarn and dyed the two

Jtem æin **kiurtil rauðr** *meðr* **kapprun** *ok æin* **blar kiurtil** *firir tolf aura.*	A red tunic together with a hood and a blue tunic for the value of 12 øre.[1]
Jtem æin **raudhr kiurtil** *ok annar* **raudhmængiadhr** *firir fiorar merkr.*	Likewise a red tunic and another of red marbled[2] cloth for a value of 4 silver marks.
Jtem æit **kapprun** *medhr* **huitum skinnum**, *ok annat medhr* **graam skinnum**, *ok thridhia medhr* **silki** *firir tyttughu aura.*	Likewise a hood lined with ermine, another lined with miniver and a third one lined with silk for 20? øre.
Jtem æin **mængiadhr mattul** *medhr* **graam skinnum** *firif fim merkr.*	Likewise a mantle of marbled cloth made with miniver, for 5 silver marks.
Jtem æit vielætz **kapprun** *medhr* **huitum skinnum** *fifir tuær merkr.*	Likewise a hood of violet cloth made with ermine, for 2 silver marks.
Jtem æin **graskinna hufa** *firir mork.*	Likewise a fur cap made of miniver for 1 silver mark.
Jtem æin **kiurtil blamængiadr** *firir tuær merkr.*	Likewise a blue marbled tunic for 2 silver marks.
Jtem æin **lodh** *firir fiorar merkr.*	Likewise a decorative piece for 4 silver marks.[3]
Jtem æin **raudmængiadhr mattul** *medhr* **graam skinnum** *ok safal firir sæx merkr.*	Likewise a red marbled mantle made with miniver and decorative trimmings[4] for 6 marks.
Jtem tiu kyr firir tiu merkr.	Likewise 10 cows for 10 silver marks.[5]
Jtem æit sylfr bælti stændh sæx aura firir tuær merkr.	Likewise a silver belt for the value of 6 øre and 2 silver marks.
Jtem fim **hauudh dukar** *firir halfa mork.*	Likewise five head veils for half a mark.
Jtem **skaut** *firir tuær merkr.*	Likewise a head covering for 2 silver marks.
Jtem tuær sylgiur gylltar er standa halfre /oe/rtogh minna en sæx aura firir fiorar merkr.	Likewise two gilded ring brooches for an ørtug less than 4 silver marks.
Jtem æin bunadr brændz sylfrs gylltr firir fiorir merkr.	Likewise a large clasp made of gilded silver for 4 silver marks.[6]
Jtem æit **syrkot mæng**[*iat firir tu*]*ær merkr.*	Likewise a supertunic of marbled cloth for 2 silver marks.[7]

[1] Aura/øre = currency.

[2] Marbled cloth refers to multicoloured or mixed cloth, often made by using two different colours of shades for warp and weft.

[3] A *lad* refers to a decorative piece or trimming, usually made of embroidery, pearls or small metal pieces (bezants). This must have been a costly piece as it had the same value as two tunics.

[4] *Safal* possibly refers to the small silver bezants used to decorative borders on garments. Sometimes safal is translated sable fur, in that case this mantle must have been lined with miniver and trimmed with sable.

[5] This entry is included in the list for comparison; the mantle mentioned above for instance has the same value as five cows.

[6] *Brænz/brase/bratz* refer to a purely ornamental type of round clasp/large bezant.

[7] Over-garment worn over a tunic, could be with or without sleeves.

Fig. 7.4: Inventory of the outfit of Ingebjørg Ivarsdatter, at her marriage to Thorleif Sigurdssøn in Vaagen, Norway, 25th of July 1335. The words relating to dress and clothing are highlighted. (Transcription and English translation by Camilla Luise Dahl)

1) Propter tria peccata plaga venit super regnum, scilicet propter superbiam et incontinenciam et cupiditatem. Et ideo Deus placari potest per tria, ut tempus plage abbreuietur.	1) It is for the sake of three sins that the plague has come on our kingdom; these are vanity, gluttony and lust. And therefore God must be soothed through three things to shorten this time of torment.
2) Primum est, quod omnes assumant veram humilitatem in vestibus, habendo vestes moderatas, non nimis longas more feminarum nec nimis strictas more scurrarum nec scissurras et fissuras vestium dispendiosas et vanas et inutiles, quia talia displicent Deo.	2) The first is to assume modesty in dress and only wear suitable garments: not too long as the women do, nor shortened and tight like the fools of fashion wear. Nor should their garments be too fitted, slashed or cut for the body for the sake of boasting, as such are superfluous, vain and excessive and displease God greatly.
3) Corpora eciam sua sic honeste gerant, ut nec prominenciora appareant, quam Deus creauit ea, propter ostentacionem, nec breuiora vel subtiliora per aliquas ligaturas vel nodos vel similia artificia, set omnia sint ad utilitatem et honorem Dei.	3) They should also keep their bodies in a proper and demure condition in order not to appear boastingly as if they were made of more: "greater" and "better" than God created them, but also not as if they were less: frail and weakened because of lacing, buttons, knots and other false things. Instead clothes should be useful, sensible and honourable to God.
4) Mulieres eciam deponant vestes ostentacionis, quas propter superbiam et vanam gloriam assupserunt, quia dyabolus dictauit mulieribus contempnentibus mores patrie sue antiquos et laudabiles quandam nouam abusionem et ornamenta indecencia in capitibus et pedibus et reliquis membris ad prouocandum luxuriam et irritandum Deum.	4) The women ought to rid themselves of their revealing and showy garments that they wear for the sake pride and vanity, thus for the women who have abandoned their old customs the Devil has invented new ill-fitting and deforming wear for head, feet and other limbs to promote lust and provoke God.

Fig. 7.5: Extract of Saint Bridget of Sweden's revelation, mid-14th century. (Transcription and English translation by Camilla Luise Dahl)

sets in different shades of green. My teacher showed me how to calculate the number of threads per cm for the warp and weft – with her method, it was 8 threads in both directions. During the weaving process, I mistakenly pulled the batten too hard and the thread count in the weft increased. My teacher corrected this and said that the fabric would feel like upholstery when it was finished. The after-treatment was also done with advice from the teacher. I wanted to wash the textile in the washing machine but again she was surprised by my method and suggested I had the fabric steam dried. Today I know that I actually had been on the right track in some ways.

The following year, I had the opportunity of studying archaeological textile fragments from deposits in the medieval town of Lödöse in Sweden. At the same time, I studied at the Weaving School in Borås, Sweden, and had learned how to analyse old textiles and translate that information into a reconstruction using contemporary materials and tools. This gave me the knowledge that medieval textiles actually had the same feel as upholstery fabrics and that the fabrics should be much denser and have a higher thread count than the fabric I had woven earlier. Of course, the material in Lödöse consisted of many different kinds of textiles and it was almost impossible to find two identical fragments. However, as I worked with the material groups, one group especially caught my attention: textiles woven in the 2/1 twill with z-spun warp and s-spun weft, often darker warp and lighter weft. The warp was always thinner and harder spun than the weft, and the thread count was always around 12–14 threads per cm in warp and 8–10 threads per cm in weft. Another factor I noted was the importance of wool types and fibre qualities. After these studies, I realized how my Herjolfsnes fabric really should have looked and felt (Vestergaard Pedersen 2003; 2004a; Hammarlund and Vestergaard Pedersen 2007).

The dress I made was cut in the Herjolfsnes pattern but with some modifications. After testing the pattern a few times, it was obvious that the pattern had to be changed to fit a modern person and, of course, some contemporary ideals about waistlines and extra width played a role in order to obtain a satisfying result. Reflections about a possible practical function of the dress were really difficult to take into account as there is no

Fig. 7.6: The author's reconstruction of Herjolfsnes dress. (© Kathrine Vestergaard Pedersen)

information about the person who wore the dress or the purpose for its uneven cut. I moved the central gore in front and back down and adjusted the side gores so the width first began from the hips and not the waistline. As seen in the mural painting, the bodice has in some cases been close-fitted to the body. Then I added lacing to the bodice and under sleeves which were lined with linen. All seams were sewn with linen thread, but should probably have been done in woollen thread as in the textiles from Lödöse. As additional clothing, I made an under-tunic of unbleached linen and an apron and head veil of finer, bleached linen. A friend made a belt, needle case and metal tips for the laces, and shoes based on a find from Stege in Møn, Denmark (Fig. 7.6).

The completed costume was an attempt to test how difficult a job it would be to make everything by hand. None of the observations, however, can be used directly in comparison with medieval material; it was merely my own experience and ability that was my reference point. Making my own medieval clothing has opened my eyes to what I have to look for and register in the archaeological material, and the process has also made it clear that however extensive the source material, there will always be 'black holes' and details that the sources do not reveal.

ACKNOWLEDGMENTS

I would like to thank Camilla Luise Dahl for her help with the written sources and illustrations.

BIBLIOGRAPHY

Bolvig, A. (2003) Dragt, magt og afmagt i danske kalkmalerier. In A. Hedeager Krag (ed.) *Dragt og magt.* Copenhagen, Museum Tusculanums Forlag, 170–189.

Crowfoot, E., F. Pritchard and K. Staniland (2001) *Textiles and Clothing c. 1150–c. 1450: Medieval finds from Excavations in London.* Woodbrige, Boydell & Brewer.

Dahl, C. L. (2005) Skriftlige vidnedsbyrd som kilde til middelalderdragt: problemer knyttet til typologi, terminologi og klædningsbestemmelse i dragtforskningen. In C. Oksen (ed.) *Middelalderdragter, Seks arbejdspapirer 2001–2005. Work Papers – Tekstilforskning på Middelaldercentret* 1. Nykøbing, 25–38.

Dahl, C. L. (forthcoming) *Dragt og pragt i middelalderen. Skrift og billedkilder til kvinders klædedragt i Norden, ca. 1325–1410.*

Geijer, A., A.-M. Franzén and M. Nockert (1994) *Drottning Margaretas gyllene kjortel i Uppsala domkyrka.* Stockholm, Kungl. Vitterhets Historie och Antikvitetes Akademien.

Gjessing, G. (1938) Skjoldehamndrakten. En senmiddelaldersk Nordnorsk Mannsdrakt, *Viking. Tidsskrift for norrøn arkeologi* 2, 27–81.

Hald, M. (1980) *Ancient Danish Textiles from Bogs and Burials, A Comparative Study of Costume and Iron Age Textiles.* Copenhagen, National Museum of Denmark.

Hammarlund, L. and K. Vestergaard Pedersen (2007) Textile appearance and visual impression – Craft knowledge applied to archaeological textiles. In A. Rast-Eicher and R. Windler (eds) *Nesat IX. Archäologische Textilfunde – Archaeological Textiles, Braunwald, 18.–21. Mai 2005.* Ennenda, ArcheoTex, 213–219.

Maik, J. (1998) Westeuropäische Wollgewebe im mittelalterlichen Elblag (Elbing). In L. Bender-Jørgensen and C. Rinaldo (eds) *Textiles in European Archaeology. Report from the 6th Nesat Symposium 7–11th May 1966 in Borås. Nesat VI.* Gotarc series A. 1, 215–231.

Nockert, M. (1997) *Bockstensmannen och hans dräkt*. Hamlstad och Varberg, Stiftelsen Hallands Länsmuseer.

Nørlund, P. (1924) Buried Norsemen at Herjolfsnes: An Archaeological and Historical Study. *Meddelelser om Grønland* 67, 87–192.

Ostergård, E. (1987) Nordboernes tøj – dagligdragten i middelalderen. In B. Wittgen (ed.) *Textila Tekniker i Nordisk Tradition. Rapport från nordiskt symposium om textila tekniker 1986*. Etnolore 6, Uppsala, Etnologiska institutionen (University of Uppsala), 95–104.

Ostergård, E. (2004) *Woven into the Earth. Textiles from Norse Greenland*. Aarhus, Århus University Press.

Saxtorph, N. M. (1997) *Danmarks kalkmalerier*. Copenhagen, Politikens Forlag.

Vedeler, M. (2004) Er dette rester av klær? Problemer knyttet til funksjonsbestemmelse av arkeologiske tekstiler. *Collegium Medievale* 17, 56–77.

Vestergaard Pedersen, K. (2003) *Middelalderlige tekstiler – en læringsproces i analyse, undersøgelse og bearbejdning af arkæologiske tekstiler efter en håndværkers metoder*. Unpublished thesis in Textile Science, University College of Borås, Sweden.

Vestergaard Pedersen, K. (2004a) *Textile production in Northern Europe 1100–1500. A Study of textiles from Lödöse and Lübeck, and a discussion of the relationship between textiles, loom-types and organization of production*. Unpublished Master's thesis in Medieval Archaeology, Aarhus University, Denmark.

Vestergaard Pedersen, K. (2004b) Den røde frakke fra Herjolfsnes. *Tenen* 2, 22–23.

Chapter 8

Tailored Criticism: The Use of Renaissance and Baroque Garments as Sources of Information

Cecilia Aneer

Understanding the information that historical dress can contribute to modern research requires an awareness of the influences that may affect how we read and interpret the remains of the past. An object with a lifespan of several hundred years does not speak with one voice about how it was originally manufactured or used, but carries traces of its life up until today. When using objects as sources of information, one important critical aspect lies in seeing through the layers of history, and another, in understanding how personal experiences may affect what we see and how we choose to interpret it.

Keywords: Renaissance, Baroque, museum, theory, reuse, conservation, burial garments.

The number of surviving garments from the Renaissance and Baroque era is significantly higher than from earlier centuries and thus provides a more extensive base for studies of dress-related questions. We know that as objects, these garments hold a great deal of information, but we have to take special care to read and understand them correctly. We need to be aware of the limitations of the surviving textile material: Which objects have survived? Why have these survived? What might have happened to them since the time when they were manufactured and first used? And how does this affect their use as sources of knowledge? In this chapter, I consider some aspects of using these extant garments as sources of information, and discuss how the researcher's own experiences may influence the approach and interpretation of the material sources and thus affect the results of the study.

EXTANT GARMENTS IN STUDIES OF HISTORICAL DRESS

By examining how surviving garments have been used in publications on dress history, we can identify a number of different ways of their use. In their simplest form, pictures of garments are used as illustrations. In these studies, images of surviving garments, alongside other materials, provide visual examples of the outlines of fashion for the period at hand. This practice is often found in literature on the history of fashion, but may also be found in historical studies of dress based on written material. We have also other cases, where in order to visualize the garments described in documents, extant objects from the same period, with similar material, ornamentation or colours have been used as examples, even though most of them have no connection to the wardrobes under examination. This happens for instance, when discussing the wardrobe contents of royalty and the nobility described in inventories and testaments. Furthermore, we have cases where the garments themselves are the objects of study, the central point of the examination. This approach has been used in many studies of surviving costumes or garments that concentrate on the manufacture and use of clothes. In theoretical terms, one can say that when an object contributes with information that helps answering the questions relevant to the examination, the object works as a source. In studies of the cut or the sewing techniques, surviving garments have frequently been used as sources (see Ringgaard in this volume). We can also use the knowledge of surviving garments as the basis for interpreting the information in contemporary written and pictorial sources.

Many studies treating surviving garments from the Renaissance and Baroque periods are based on examinations of single garments or costumes from one specific collection. In these studies, the garments usually work as study-objects and other textiles, pictures and written sources are used to cast light on the historical context of the object under investigation. We, however, very rarely use Renaissance and Baroque garments as direct sources, as surviving garments are relatively sparse and geographically spread.

Objects as sources of information

The information that can be derived from an object, such as a costume, is dependent on our knowledge of its history, the context in which it was manufactured, used and preserved. An isolated object, the provenance of which is unknown, may only be interpreted on the basis of its physical appearance. Materials, shape, structure, techniques, colours and elements of decoration constitute readable traces. These can give us information about the object's original appearance, field of use and manufacture, but also about the preferences of the users, both individual and cultural. An object may also show traces of wear, spots, colour changes, repair and adjustments, which can give us information of its use throughout history. If we wish to use an object as a source of scientific study, knowledge about when and where it was made or used is generally needed. When an object lacks provenance, we can usually date and link it to a cultural and social setting by comparing its physical data with other surviving garments, pictures or texts with a known history. An isolated object may work as an example, an illustration and a complement to other sources or as a single study-object.

However, when we use these items as sources, it is most common to study them within a context, as an element in a group of similar objects from the same time or place, or as a part of a group with different objects from the same region. By comparing several surviving garments from the same period we can for instance draw conclusions about the use of materials and technical solutions characteristic of a certain period, or variations in use. We can also see how their manufacture or use has changed over time by comparing garments from the same geographical area but different periods. If the garments are instead studied as part of a larger textile production and compared with other textiles from the same period, we are able to make hypotheses about patterns of thought, for example how economic values were regarded in comparison to aesthetic ones. An example of this can be seen when comparing extant Renaissance garments, embroideries and textiles for interior decoration. Within each category one can see a characteristic way of saving fabric by joining smaller pieces together. This practice occurs in simple objects as well as in items intended for royalty and nobility. These seams are possible evidence of an economical approach within the textile trade, where the value of the fabrics was regarded as more important than the negative effect the seams would have on the aesthetic impression. Most historical studies of dress are built upon a combination of different kinds of sources, where the interaction between different pieces of information helps us to see things more clearly and pose new questions.

THE REMAINS OF AN ERA – WHAT SURVIVED AND WHY

The surviving garments from the 16th and 17th centuries are relatively few and are today in the care of several smaller and larger collections mainly in Europe and North America. Most of these collections contain only a few garments each. The limited material sometimes makes it hard for us to determine the date of manufacture or to uncover the provenance and authenticity of an object. An important starting-point for understanding these garments is to try to get a picture of what objects are still extant, which factors have contributed to their preservation and which changes they might have undergone up until today.

Many of the Renaissance and Baroque garments seen in museums today have been used as funeral garments and have been recovered from graves. Views on how to treat the remains of the dead have varied through the centuries and in different geographical areas. During the 18th and 19th centuries, many funeral garments were incorporated in museum collections when tombs were opened for examination. Since the last century, it has been more common to document the garments carefully when graves are opened, but the costumes are often put back in the graves after the work is finished. When we work with funeral costumes it is important to keep in mind that in the 16th and 17th centuries, there were several variations in the customs of dressing the dead. Garments that had been used in life could be reused as funeral garments, or new ones could be made. Garments taken from the wardrobe of the deceased are usually distinguished by the characteristic interlinings and tailoring of the period. Garments made especially for the funeral ceremony may have been cut in resemblance to fashion, made of the same fabrics and with the same decorations, but without the interlinings that were essential for the fashionable silhouette. These garments could also be open in the back to make the dressing of the deceased easier.

During the 17th century, a specific funerary fashion developed. It consisted of a long, wide coat-like garment with a quite wide three-quarter or full-length sleeve. The garment was open at the front, from collar to hem, and closed with a row of bows of silk ribbon. These garments were predominantly used for men and children.

Several costumes and garments from the 16th and 17th centuries have been preserved because they have been linked to famous persons or events by tradition. The Sture suits in Uppsala Cathedral, Sweden, constitute one such example (Fig. 8.1). These costumes were worn by Svante, Nils and Erik Sture, three members of a prominent Swedish noble family. They were accused of high treason and were executed at Uppsala Castle in 1567. The widow, Märta Sture, put the garments in a chest, which was then placed in the family burial chapel where the clothes have been kept and shown to visitors through the centuries.

We also have examples of how the wish to connect garments to famous persons has sometimes led to misinterpretations. Thus, the provenance and date of several objects have been reassessed in later years. In the *Catalogue of English Domestic Embroidery* from 1938, J. L. Nevinson suggests such a revision. Nevinson discusses a pair of gloves that by tradition is said to have belonged to Henry VIII of England (1491–1547). The gloves have high, embroidered cuffs of a kind that were not in fashion before the beginning of the 17th century and which were especially popular between 1610 and 1630. The embroidery shows a combination of roses and thistles, the symbols of the English and Scottish royal families. The ornamentation shows a symbolic tie to the pictorial language of the Stuart family often used in the early years of the 17th century. Therefore Nevinson questions the likelihood of the gloves having belonged to Henry VIII (Nevinson 1938, 95).

The oldest collections we have containing several costumes from the same period and social setting date from the second half of the 16th and first half of the 17th centuries. Most of these are the remains of royal or princely wardrobes, which have been preserved in close relation to the places where they were manufactured and used. At the royal courts, other pieces of material dealing with the production and use of clothing have also been saved. There are accounts, inventories and letters that can help us understand the context within which the garments should be seen and interpreted. Collections of this kind have survived from the Swedish, Danish and Saxon courts.

The economical value of the textile materials was the basis for an extensive reuse of both fabrics and materials for decoration. Both garments and textiles for interior decoration were reused within the secular as well as the ecclesiastical sphere. These remains of costumes are nowadays often found in church vestments. A chasuble or priestly vestment and an altar frontal in *Storkyrkan* in Stockholm are examples of this. These are made from the cloak of a costume ordered by Swedish King Charles X Gustav in Paris for his coronation in 1654. The vestments were given to the church in 1705 by Queen Hedwig Eleonora.

Several garments from the Renaissance and Baroque seem to have been preserved because of their splendid materials and skilled craftsmanship. These objects have

Fig. 8.1: Eric Sture's Suit, Uppsala Cathedral, Sweden. (The Royal Armoury, Stockholm; Photo: Göran Schmidt)

impressed contemporary as well as later generations. They are often found on their own and usually lack provenance. Often they are small items like gloves and nightcaps or single larger garments such as doublets or shirts, but very seldom are they complete costumes. Some groups of garments seem to derive from a specific geographic area, such as the embroidered linen jackets and caps from the first half of the 17th century, so numerous in the British Isles. The interest in collecting historical objects, especially in the late 19th century, led to a widespread trade in, among other things, Renaissance and Baroque textiles. Many garments reached private and public collections through auctions during that period, and in this process, knowledge of their history was often lost.

Limitations of the material

Nearly all of the garments discussed thus far originate from the highest levels of society, from royalty and nobility, and are not representative of the population as a whole. Very few garments from the lower levels of society have survived. These are usually smaller or singular pieces of dress that have been recovered from excavations, on sunken ships or concealed in historical buildings. The woollen garments more common among poorer people are extremely few, probably because these often were reused until they were worn out. Damage from moths and other pests have also largely reduced the amount of woollen garments from the nobility and royal courts.

Another imbalance in existing material is in the relationship between the number of male and female garments, where the male ones are considerably more numerous than the female ones. There may be many reasons for this situation, but a couple of these can be found in the circumstances of preservation discussed above. Several of the garments that have survived because of their history can be linked to monarchs, high ranking military officers or known politicians, who at the time were usually men. Another important explanation can be found in the reuse of material. Garments which consist of many relatively small parts, are more frequent among the surviving material than others. The male doublets constitute one of the largest groups among the extant Renaissance and Baroque garments, while breeches, cloaks and skirts, which contained larger pieces of fabric easier to reuse, are very scarce.

When we examine the more extensive royal or princely collections, we can see that there are more garments from some periods than from others. For instance, there are more extant garments from the 1620s and 1630s than from the period between 1640 and 1670. This might have an economical explanation. During the 1620s and 1630s, brocades seem to have been less usual and plain silks were used instead as a base for patterning with pinking, braids, woven bands or embroidery. Around 1640, a new form of aesthetics was introduced, which used more closely patterned surfaces. The garments from this period were more often made of brocade or patterned with heavy metal embroidery. The metal had an actual economic value even after the garments and fabrics were worn out, and this was often melted down and recycled. The garments were not necessarily burnt in the process, as often the metal thread was taken from the garment before being melted.

The groups of extant garments discussed above thus have survived either by choice or by chance and strong, long-lived institutions such as courts and churches have been of importance for the preservation of larger groups of objects.

Dating an object

Very few garments from the 16th and 17th centuries can be dated precisely through being used or produced on a known occasion. Only a small number of garments made for and used by famous people at large ceremonies, such as coronations, weddings or funerals belong to this category. However, the fact that a garment has been used on a known occasion does not necessarily mean that it was made for it. Garments that have been reused for funerals might have been in use for many years before the burial and may have been out of fashion at the time of death.

A newly made garment may not be in the latest fashion either. There are occasions when by tradition uniformity rather than fashion seems to have been the priority for the choice of costumes. We can see an example of this in the so-called 'Polish Roll', a 15.5 m long and 28 cm wide gouache painting depicting the parade at the wedding of Sigismund III of Poland, former King of Sweden, and Konstantia of Austria in Krakow 1605 (Fig. 8.2). This painting shows different groups of people dressed in costumes fashionable in Western Europe from the 1560s up to the date of the wedding. We could easily believe that old-fashioned garments could have lived on and been worn together with more fashionable ones, but this does not seem to be the case. Instead, the dress of each group seems to follow the fashion of one given period systematically. A group of halberdiers flanking the bride's carriage wear *pluderhose* (see Fig. 8.1), ruffs and cloaks ending at the waist, in line with the German and northern European fashion of the 1560s and 1570s. Another group wears knee-length straight open breeches, cassocks with a straight waistline and falling bands, a combination that was only in fashion during a short period between 1600 and 1610. This example demonstrates the danger of dating a garment solely from cut and construction. A costume is seldom older than the fashion it mirrors, but it might be considerably younger.

Another method of dating surviving garments is through the materials. The patterning of silks and velvets, like the cut, follows the turns of fashion and may work as a starting-point for dating an object. When using this approach, we must keep in mind that the material might not have been new when the garment was made. There are examples of garments made up from fabrics that were already several hundred years old. In *Museo Stibbert* in Florence, Italy, there are some garments made of Renaissance fabrics, which were created in the 19th century, to be displayed as part of the exhibition of armour. The fabric in these objects is authentic but we have to consider the garments as being reconstructions. By combining knowledge about silk production and the changes in fashion, the probability of making an accurate dating is considerably higher.

Fig. 8.2: One section of the 'Polish Roll' depicting the parade at the wedding of King Sigismund III of Poland and Konstantia of Austria in Krakow 1605. The Royal Castle, Warsaw, Poland. ZWK/1528 (The Royal Armoury, Stockholm; Photo: Göran Schmidt)

Reconstructions made from completely new materials may also have ended up in museum collections. In certain eras of history there have been periods with a strong interest in past times, as, for example, at the end of the 19th and first decades of the 20th centuries, when the past was often recreated in masquerades, parades or by the staging of historical events. For these occasions old garments were reused or new ones made. Reconstructions of this kind have sometimes ended up in museums and been thought to be authentic historic garments. One interesting example of this is presented by Johannes Pietsch in *Zwei Schauben aus dem Bayerischen Nationalmuseum München* (2004). Pietsch examined two similar councillors' coats thought to be from the middle of the 17th century. Through careful comparison he was able to show that one of them is an original from the 17th century, while the other one is a copy. The reproduction had been modelled after the original and was probably made in the 19th century.

ALTERATIONS TO THE GARMENTS IN ORIGINAL AND LATER CONTEXTS

As we illustrate in this volume, when studying historical garments it is important to understand what changes the objects might have undergone since they were originally made and used. The changes could be divided into those made while the garments were still functioning in their original setting and those made when these were reused in new contexts. When studying garments, it is usual to find traces of changes in size, repair work or adjustments for a later fashion. The same garment has sometimes been changed on several occasions; decorations taken off and reused, worn-out linings replaced and changes made to fit new users. The recurring adjustments were a natural part of the everyday use of dress in the 16th and 17th centuries. These changes can often be recognized because the materials added are similar to the original fabrics and the proportions of the garments are kept in line with fashion. An example of changes of this kind is seen in Svante Sture's doublet in Uppsala Cathedral. Its body has been widened by the insertion of gores in the side and back seams. The added material is very similar to the original parts and the characteristic proportions of dress in the middle of the 16th century can be clearly seen.

Surviving garments dating from the Renaissance and Baroque periods have found new uses through the centuries whether as memorial objects or in theatres, masquerades or pageants. Historical garments have also been reused as models for sculptures or paintings with historical themes. In these contexts, adjustments may have been made to make them fit the purpose.

Materials and elements of decoration from Renaissance and Baroque garments have also been reused in new contexts such as interior decoration or church vestments. The materials reused in these contexts have mainly been exclusive fabrics, embroideries, decorative bands and metal lace. Material from larger objects has been re-cut and it may be hard to discern its original use. The piecing of the fabric or the character of the decorations may sometimes give a clue to earlier fields of use. From smaller garments, whole parts have often been used as decoration for instance on chasubles or chalice veils. In these cases, the garments used, such as baldrics, gauntlets or nightcaps have often been embroidered. A chalice veil in Kräcklinge Church, Närke, Sweden, decorated with the embroidered parts of a pair of early 17th century gauntlets shows this use (Fig. 8.3). These are usually easier to recognize because of their shape and the adaptation of the design to fit it, which often is characteristic to the specific groups of garments. In Scandinavia, such fragments of garments are still found in churches today.

Conservation treatment

The different uses to which the garments have been put throughout their history have worn them out and created a need for repair. Today many of these garments belong to museums where they function as historical documents, used in exhibitions to visualise past times and, in research, as sources of new knowledge. Even present day use leads to

Fig. 8.3: Chalice veil decorated with embroidered gauntlets. Kräcklinge Church, Närke, Sweden. (Photo courtesy of Riksantikvarieämbetet, Stockholm. Nr. Pietas 5029/70:2)

wear and tear, and since the beginning of the 20th century, preventive measures have been taken to keep historical costumes from further disintegration.

Conservation treatment has followed different paths through the last hundred years. At the beginning of the 20th century, the principle that the supporting materials used should be easy to distinguish from the original ones was applied. During this period, fabrics or colours differing from the original material were used for repairs. These alterations were easy to identify, but made it hard to imagine the objects' original appearance. Today many garments are given conservation treatments in relation to exhibitions so that objects give a hint of their former magnificence. Therefore, materials resembling the original, and dyed in the same colours, are usually used for repairs. For the same reason, parts of garments that have gone missing have occasionally been reconstructed. These later restorations can sometimes be hard to discover if the principles used are unfamiliar to the observer. Conservation treatment, like other changes to an object, affects the information that it can supply: supporting material may conceal the reverse of the garment and original seams may have been opened and re-sewn. Many workshops document the conservation treatments in written descriptions and sometimes also in photographs. These reports constitute an important base for us in discovering and dating changes to garments.

Most extant garments from the Renaissance and Baroque have undergone more than one conservation treatment during the 20th century. An example can be seen in the costume worn by Swedish King Gustavus Adolphus when he was wounded at the battle of Kleinwerder (Poland) in 1627. This costume has been kept in the Royal Armoury at Stockholm Castle since the 1620s and has been shown to visitors through the years (Figs 8.4–8.5). It was first conserved in the Pietas workshop, Stockholm, in 1911. At this time the pinked silk satin of the doublet was falling apart and the sleeves were hanging in rags. The metal bands of the breeches had come loose from the fabric in several places. During conservation, the fragmentary silk of the doublet was fixed to a supporting fabric of shantung silk and the bands of the breeches re-sewn. In 1975, after several years in different exhibitions, the garments were once again in need of con-servation treatment to be able to withstand further exposure. On this occasion more radical changes were made. The doublet was given a new outer fabric of silk satin, which was sewn on over the fragments of the original one, and the decoration bands were attached onto the new surface. The breeches were taken apart by opening parts of the seams at the crotch and on the inside legs. The outer fabric, interlining and lining were treated separately and rejoined afterwards (Fig. 8.6). Those metal bands which had gone missing through the years, were replaced by cotton ones. In both these conservation tasks

Fig. 8.4: Costume worn by the Swedish King Gustavus Adolphus at the Battle of Kleinwerder (Poland) in 1627, before the conservation treatment in 1911. (The Royal Armoury, Stockholm, Sweden. LRK 3849 & 3375; Photo: unknown)

Fig. 8.5: Costume worn by the Swedish King Gustavus Adolphus at the Battle of Kleinwerder (Poland) in 1627, after conservation treatment 1976–78. (The Royal Armoury, Stockholm, Sweden. LRK 3849 & 3375; Photo: Göran Schmidt)

Fig. 8.6: Detail of costume worn by the Swedish King Gustavus Adolphus at the Battle of Kleinwerder (Poland) in 1627, during the conservation treatment 1976–78. (The Royal Armoury, Stockholm, Sweden. LRK 3849 & 3375; Photo: Göran Schmidt)

new material was added, and in the last one, some of the original seams were replaced by new ones. If we are to distinguish the original parts of a garment from later changes and estimate when an alteration has taken place, it is important to learn about differences in materials and technical solutions from various periods.

USE OF EXPERIENCE IN STUDIES OF HISTORICAL GARMENTS

We can describe knowledge in various ways. On a basic level, it is usual to talk about having an objectivistic or a relativistic approach to information. If we see knowledge in an objectivistic way, one single truth is thought to exist. With a relativistic approach, knowledge is thought to be dependent upon the individual and the cultural context within which it is produced and applied. When working from a relativistic point of view, it is important for us to be aware of the factors that may have an effect on the results of the examination. The experience of the researcher is thought to, consciously or unconsciously, influence the choice of questions and sources, the methods of documentation and analysis, and the presentation of the results. To enable other scholars to form an opinion about the reliability of the results, it is important that we make the examination transparent. That is, it is important to supply information about not just the outcome, but also the research process, the way of thinking and the critical observations related to the sources that influenced the paths we chose and the conclusions we drew.

Our experience may consist of knowledge we have gleaned from our education or from fieldwork, but may also include everything else learned from everyday life. A researcher's experience can be of a collective or an individual quality. Collective experiences may constitute common knowledge among those who have studied a university subject, grown up under a certain period in time or lived in the same country. The individual experiences might consist of specialist knowledge from a specific field such as skill in a craft. The experience can therefore be of both a practical and theoretical nature, and obtained through practice or theoretical studies. All experiences gathered by an individual constitute the frame within which the world can be understood and interpreted. The experience can be used at different points in an examination; it may work as a base for documentation, as a tool for analysis or as a foundation for practical experiments to test the reliability of hypotheses and conclusions.

Experiences are tied to the culture, social setting and period in time where they have been made. This means that they cannot be directly transferred to a source from another time or culture. The first encounter with an object from another period or culture often triggers unexpected reactions, as the impressions do not fit into the researcher's frame of experience. My first close examination of a Renaissance garment caused such a reaction. At the time, I thought that the object was very carelessly made. In my eyes the threads were too thick and the stitches in the seams were very uneven. On this occasion, my experience of Renaissance garments consisted of information from literature, and the sewing was not usually mentioned there. My reaction was instead based on my own experience of sewing, which came from a modern tailoring education. Much of the tailoring taught today is based on an ideal that was developed during the 19th century. During this period, great importance was placed upon a perfect finish, including thin threads and short, even stitching. From the middle of the 19th century, hand-sewing had to compete with the sewing machine. This meant a rationalization for the trade, but it also changed some of the established technical solutions since the abilities of the machine were more limited than manual work (see Ringgaard in this volume). The Renaissance garments also struck me as very heavy compared to today's fashions. Now we require garments to be flexible and easy to move in, which affects the design, the choice of materials and the technical solutions. The properties which have been preferred in clothing have varied from one period to another and are connected to cultural trends such as the attitude to representation or activity. My reaction on my first encounter with a Renaissance garment was the result of a lack of experience of clothing from this period. Many of the features I found different and hard to understand at the time appear as typical for their context when I see them today.

When objects are used as sources, the experience of extant material is very important. By studying a large number of objects we obtain knowledge of what is typical, and how variations in their appearance and technical solutions have developed. Among collectors of antiquities the term 'connoisseurship' has long been used to describe this type of experience-based knowledge and in archaeology, the expression 'pottery sense' has been used. When working with a small and geographically widespread group of objects, such as Renaissance or Baroque costumes, we often have to complement object studies with information about garments published in books. The same critical approach should be applied to these sources. To understand the objects in relation to the culture in which they were produced and used, we also need to have general knowledge of the period under study.

Levels of experience

The level of knowledge within a field may also be of significance for visual and sensual impressions. When we encounter an object of a well-known type, the impressions often confirm knowledge we already have at hand. It is easy to see that the things we know how to look for and the technical aspects we have learnt are typical for a group of objects. Details never observed before may, on the other hand, pass unnoticed. Beginners in the field do not know what to expect and hence often see other things than someone with previous knowledge. Our experience can thus work as a lens focusing on the information of an object, but at the same time limit the sensibility to details outside our frame of experience. Experience within a field can exist at different levels, which can have consequences for how the researcher approaches the primary sources. At a basic level it is possible to speak of unprofessional, educated and professional experiences. When discussing the experience in a craft practised by an amateur, he or she may know the basic techniques from books and practice. The educated person has been trained in a professional approach to the work, requiring knowledge about materials and technical skills as well as estimating the cost of the work and interacting with costumers. The professional may in addition have experience of how the knowledge is altered in the light of changing requirements, working conditions and technical development (see Nørgaard in this volume). These different points of view influence both the questions that arise in our meeting with an object and the conclusions we draw from it.

CONCLUSIONS

The surviving garments from the Renaissance and Baroque periods have many limitations. They are relatively few and geographically widespread. Only a small number of objects can be dated without comparison to other sources. The clothes still extant have been kept for different reasons and are not representative of all strata of society. Quite a large part consists of male garments from the highest echelon of society, items of the more splendid and costly kind; and very few pieces can be traced back to women or people from the lower end of society. Some garments have an exciting history, which has been of importance for their preservation. Others have been concealed and found in later times. Parts of garments have also been reused and have survived as elements of other objects. Most of the surviving garments have been changed through the centuries. An awareness of the potential and limitations of sources is the base for acquiring new knowledge. All types of sources have their weaknesses, but by knowing them it is also possible to identify what questions the material can possibly answer. The information supplied by the objects is directly dependent on the experiences of the researcher and the cultural frames within which he or she works. Besides knowledge about the limitations of the sources, for a critical approach, we also need an understanding of the reasons for the choice of material and interpretations on which the results are based. By consciously thinking of how one's own experiences relate to the pattern of thought and technical knowledge of the period under study, it is easier to avoid mistakes when it comes to the interpretation of the information supplied by the objects.

BIBLIOGRAPHY

On the topic of Renaissance and Baroque dress, the following titles give an introduction to surviving material in the form of patterns taken from extant garments, photographic illustrations and documentary descriptions.

Arnold, J. (1985) *Patterns of Fashion. The cut and construction of clothes for men and women c. 1560–1620.* London, Macmillan.

Flamand Christensen, S. (1940) De Danske Kongers Kronologiske Samling paa Rosenborg. *Kongedragterne fra 17. og 18. Aarhundrede.* Vol. I–II, Copenhagen, Munksgaard.

Hart, A. and S. North (1998) *Historical Fashion in Detail. The 17th and 18th Centuries.* London, V & A Publications.

Rangström, L. (2002) *Modelejon. Manligt mode 1500-tal 1600-tal 1700-tal.* Stockholm, Livrustkammaren and Bokförlaget Atlantis.

Stolleis, K. (1977) *Die Gewänder aus der Lauinger Fürstengruft.* München, Bayerisches Nationalmuseum and Deutscher Kunstverlag.

Other major works dealing with dress in the Renaissance and Baroque era are:

Alcega, J. de (1979) *Tailor's Pattern Book 1589*, Carlton, (Bedford), Ruth Bean Publishers. Facsimile from a Spanish original, *Libero de Geometria, Pratica y Traca,* published in Madrid 1589.

Arnold, J. (1988) *Queen Elizabeth's Wardrobe Unlock'd.* Leeds, Maney.

Zander-Seidel, J. (1990) *Textiler Hausrat. Kleidung und Haustextilien in Nürnberg von 1500–1650.* München, Deutscher Kunstverlag.

In this chapter, the following works have been used:

Arnold, J. (1973) Dating Costume from Construction Techniques. Chapter II in *A Handbook of Costume*. London, Macmillan, 129–146.

Baumgarten, L. (1998) Altered Historical Clothing. *Dress* 25, 42–57.

Bergman, E. (1956) Begravningskläderna. In M. Olsson (ed.) *Vasagraven i Uppsaladomkyrka*. Stockholm, Nord. Rotogravyr, 155–177.

Estham, I. (1989) *Kungligt – kyrkligt*. Stockholm, Husgerådskammaren.

Nevinson, J. L. (1938) *Catalogue of English Domestic Embroidery*. London, Victoria & Albert Museum.

Pietsch, J. (2004) *Zwei Schauben aus dem Bayerischen Nationalmuseum München: Ein Beitrag zur Kostümforschung*. München, Anton Siegl Verlag.

Pylkkänen, R. (1955) Gravdräkter från 1600-talet i Åbo domkyrkomuseum. In *Åbostads Historiska Museums årsskrift*, 17–18, Åbo.

Swartling-Andersson, M. (2000) Tröja och byxor burna av Gustav II Adolf i 30-åriga kriget. In I. Wallenborg (ed.) *Textila skatter i svenska museer. Konservatorer berättar*, Udevalla, Svenska föreningen för textilkonservering, 109–114.

Chapter 9

Costume in a Museological Context: Dealing with Costume and Dress from Modern Danish History

Tove Engelhardt Mathiassen and Helle Leilund

In this chapter, the authors, who are both museum curators, discuss how different academic perspectives and approaches have influenced the content of dress and textile collections from Modern Danish history. This is illustrated by looking at how the Danish Open Air Museum in Århus made its choices when reconstructing historical dresses for a Living History project, and collecting wedding outfits from the last 50 years.

Keywords: reconstruction, painting, museology, museum collections, wedding clothes, national identity, modern history, historical dress.

Compared to earlier historical periods, Modern Danish history is rich in the number and variety of historical sources on textile and costume. In a museological context, this period is chronologically defined from the beginning of the Absolute Monarchy in 1660 to the present day, in other words, the last 350 years. In general, the history of this period is quite well documented: our knowledge of and insight into the different social and cultural groups and individuals, materials, techniques and production are quite comprehensive due to the abundance of preserved objects and other types of historical sources in archives, museums and libraries. Yet, this does not always make it simple to work with modern costume, dress and textiles. Here the problem is not the scarcity of sources and knowledge, rather the challenge is of quite another kind.

The rich sources, the variety of academic disciplines that focus on dress or dress-related subjects as their object of research, as well as the large number of theoretical and methodological approaches available, make the study of modern dress and textile a somewhat complex matter. All in all, it means that it is very important to be aware of what you are doing and how you do it, if you want to study dress in a historical and cultural context. An analysis of modern dress and textile should demonstrate not only a critical and conscious approach to the sources, but also knowledge of the scientific or academic context of the analysis. Furthermore, an analysis should illustrate that you think critically of your own academic practice as well.

In the following pages we examine, discuss and exemplify important considerations when analysing dress from modern history and working with the reconstruction of historical costumes in a museological context.

SO MANY SOURCES....

The storerooms and exhibitions of many Danish museums include a large number of costumes and textiles from this period, often collected over a long period of time. These concrete preserved material objects are one of the main sources of information for textile and dress history. Historical costumes may inform us about colour and materials, the cut of clothes in different historical periods, and different techniques. Often, we would also like the dresses in the museum storerooms to enlighten us as to how different people in society were dressed on different occasions; and sometimes we use dresses to learn about a specific style or designer. A historical costume can be asked many different questions, depending on the type of information you wish to focus on. Usually, it is not possible to communicate directly with the person who once owned and wore the preserved dress in a museum storeroom, to ask how the dress was made, how and when it was used and how it felt to wear it, since this person is probably not alive anymore. Nevertheless, it is possible to get a sense of a human body and of a life lived in a dress once worn that no other type of preserved material object from the past might provide. For dresses are always connected to people.

Even though costumes in museum storerooms can tell fascinating and very diverse stories about the people of the past, there is a great deal of knowledge that the material object in itself cannot provide. As a textile or fashion designer, you might let yourself be inspired by and adopt a single detail you discover in a historic costume. Yet, as a person working with the reconstruction of historical dress or someone wanting to understand how and why dresses looked like they did, were produced or were worn, at a certain place or time, in a certain social or cultural environment, you will have to consider a broader historical, social and cultural context.

Preserved historical costumes and dresses – material objects – are just one type of source; there are many equally important sources to enlighten us on the cultures of dress and costume from Modern Danish history. Pictures, such as paintings, drawings and prints are essential sources for the study of dress history, particularly of the 17th, 18th and the beginning of the 19th century, where other types of sources are limited. However, it is important to be critical of artists: they are free to some extent to paint whatever they want. Another problem with art as a source of dress history is that paintings especially tend to illustrate the clothes of society's most fashionable people of higher ranks and good income, since ordinary people seldom had a portrait painted of themselves (Fig. 9.1). Common people in their daily wear appear rarely on paintings until the end of the 19th century,

Fig. 9.1: The Fenger Family Portrait *painted by Ulrich Ferdinandt Beenfeldt, 1769. (Courtesy of the National Museum of Denmark; Photo: Peter Danstrøm)*

when it became a popular theme among certain artists who were engaged in exposing social inequality and the conditions among poorer people in Danish society. Thus, they painted manual workers, everyday life among peasants and people who lived in workhouses (Fig. 9.2).

Other examples of early pictorial sources of fashionable dress are printed fashion plates and fashion magazines. From the 18th century onwards, these were printed in Paris and distributed all over Europe (Andersen 1977). Today they constitute an important source to those who analyze fashion or wish to theorize on how and why a specific style may have evolved or spread socially or geographically (see Ringgaard in this volume).

Photography, which was invented in the middle of the 19th century, today has become one of the most valued pictorial sources in documenting all types of costume. In the early years of photography, not everyone could afford to have their picture taken, but compared to earlier historic periods, private photographs, as well as professional fashion photographs and documentary pictures in newspapers give dress historians great insight into the appearance and use of dress among larger and more socially and culturally differentiated groups of people (Fig. 9.3).

Pictures – drawings and photographs – in fashion magazines, in household books on sewing and all kinds of warehouse catalogues are other essential pictorial sources of modern dress. From the 20th century onwards, cinema and television have played a

Fig. 9.2: At the end of the 19th century, social inequality and conditions among the poorer people in society became a popular theme among Danish artists. A beggar at the door. *Painting by Carl V. Meyer, 1910. (Courtesy of the National Museum of Denmark; Photo: Peter Danstrom)*

Fig. 9.3: From around 1860, photographs have been a valuable source of dress history. Farmer Olsen and family photographed in the late 1800s. (Courtesy of the National Museum of Denmark; Photo: Peter Danstrom)

considerable role in the communication of fashion news, as actors on the movie screen inspired and influenced fashion the world over (see Borrell in this volume).

Early written sources on dress from modern history are stored in archives and libraries and include estate inventories, letters, memories and diaries. These sources have been fundamental in analysing the history of Danish fashion in the 17th, 18th and first half of the 19th century as well as traditional dress among peasants from the same period (see, for instance, Andersen 1960; 1977; Lorenzen 1975). Studying Danish law may also be very helpful as a tool to investigate dress in the 17th and 18th century, since sumptuary laws included thorough definitions of what sort of dress the different estates in society were allowed to wear (Fig. 9.4). Novels, biographies and memoirs are other examples of written sources that often enclose detailed descriptions of dress.

Several Danish museums contain archives of collected life stories of 'ordinary' Danes, and these narratives often include remarks or descriptions of clothes, *e.g.* of the production of textiles in peasant households as well as many other related subjects.

Methods and sources are quite different for dress historians working with contemporary history since you are often able to actually communicate with those involved. Working with present-day history means for instance that you have the opportunity to enquire into how people produced, bought or used a specific type of dress. Later in this chapter, an example of documenting and collecting contemporary wedding outfits and wedding culture in the context of a cultural historic museum is discussed.

BE CRITICAL!

As we have seen throughout this volume, in dress analysis it is vital to work critically and consciously with the available source materials. Here, we illustrate one of the complexities of the field. As mentioned earlier, paintings are seen as a central source for the study of dress from the Modern period, yet it is important to keep in mind that a picture or a painting does not necessarily represent an objective truth about reality out there, as the following example demonstrates.

In 1844, Professor N. L. Høyen of The Royal Danish Art Academy urged his art students to paint not only portraits of wealthy and important social figures or mythological motives inspired by ancient Greece or Rome. Instead, he argued, art students ought to pay attention to and paint Danish landscapes and the life of the Danes. Artists should focus on national history and the characteristics of the national spirit, which Høyen believed was expressed most genuinely and truthfully among common people. The daily tasks of peasants and fishermen and what was seen as typical Danish landscapes with light beech forests became favourite subjects among Danish artists, one of whom was Julius Exner (1825–1910).

Exner, one of Høyen's students at the Academy, painted about 200 paintings during his career, many of which included peasants dressed in what were considered traditional folk costumes from different Danish localities, for example the islands of Amager and Fanø, and the Hedebo region. From 1852, he almost only painted so-called genre paintings – scenes from everyday life where human figures are seen as stereotypes and portrayed anonymously – and his works eventually became very popular. Those unable to afford an original Exner painting were offered a variety of not so costly reproductions to hang on their walls.

Even though the audience and costumiers loved him, he soon lost popularity among art critics. The latter thought the paintings to be far too naïve and sentimental. However, they never questioned his paintings as a valuable source of cultural history (Zenius 1976, 96).

Marianne Zenius has analysed Danish genre paintings and painters as a potentially valid source of cultural history (Zenius 1976). She has compared the motifs in the paintings with what we actually know of architectural style and dress among peasants, and has concluded that genre paintings are a very doubtful source. Her study demonstrates that Exner's aim was not so much to make an objective documentation of costume and interiors among people in the countryside in the 19th century, as it was to contribute in general to the creation of a public feeling of what it meant to be truly Danish and to be part of a common Danish history. The peasants and other people on Exner's paintings are usually not poor, dirty or starving; they are often happy, younger and dressed in their Sunday best. However, the problem with interpreting Exner's paintings is that people in general have been looking at them as a naïve but true representation and documentation of interiors and costume among Danish peasants in the 'old days'. Reconstructions of historical costumes and even whole buildings have been based entirely on his paintings (Fig. 9.5).

Exner constructed the rooms and dressed his figures using artistic license. He, like other genre painters, owned peasant costumes, objects and even furniture and inserted them in his paintings, sometimes changing things slightly, making people or the interior look a little richer or poorer depending on the situation. Zenius has compared paintings by Exner and found exactly the same watch, pipe and even items of the same costumes and models in different works from quite different places in the country. According to Ellen Andersen (1960), Exner, as well as another famous Danish genre painter, Christen Dalsgaard, painted costumes that were old-fashioned and no longer in use at the time of their work, or combined parts of dresses that no one probably would ever wear together. From 1850 to 1910, the period when Exner painted his pictures, most people in the Danish countryside had already stopped using colourful and home-made costumes and had adapted to a more urban dress culture. There were only a few regions left – so-called dress islands – where some older women might still have used regionally-based dress. In most parts of the country, the dress of the younger segment of the population in rural areas did not differentiate much from the dresses used among similar social groups in urban areas (Lorenzen 1975).

We must thus conclude that it is not safe to use genre paintings as a primary source for considering how people in the Danish countryside actually were dressed in the 19th century. However, if you are interested in the ideological construction of nations and nationalism, genre paintings are an excellent source!

Fig. 9.4: The illustration on the lid of a tobacco box can be an excellent and surprising source of dress history. The lid depicts the dress of the four different estates in Danish society in the 18th century. In the centre sits a nobleman wearing a typical red coat with the blue ribbon and star of the Order of the Elephant. To the left is a black-clad priest, and to the right, a member of the bourgeoisie wearing a blue coat. The man wearing a brown coat and a black hat is a peasant from Zealand. In the 1780s, peasants were the only estate not to wear wigs. Blonde, powdered wigs were fashionable among the other estates. (Courtesy of the National Museum of Denmark; Photo: Roberto Fortuna)

DIFFERENT DISCIPLINES – DIFFERENT APPROACHES

Given the fact that a number of academic disciplines study dress in this historical period, the methodological and theoretical approaches to dress analysis vary a great deal. For an academic scholar, it is possible to study dress-related subjects in the context of art history, sociology, history, anthropology, ethnology, economics and conservation. Each discipline has developed its own scientific perspective on the subject, its own methods and theoretical approaches. While students at art and design schools may give more attention to the dimension of handicraft, the concrete techniques and innovative processes in creating new design or fashion, an economist working with fashion would probably be more focused on the impact fashion has or has had on economic development – and *vice versa* – in a given industry or in society as a whole.

Art historians for instance study fashion by analysing it as an element in the history of style. In biographies or exhibitions of great designers, the perspective and focus of an art historian is often on the designer as artist: his work, his oeuvre, his contributions to fashion history. Questions that are not so interesting from this analytical perspective are who used or produced the garments made by the great designer, and were these dresses available generally or only for the chosen few.

The social and cultural sciences, like sociology, anthropology, ethnology and history also study fashion, textile and dress, although emphasizing other aspects of the subject. The approaches differ: history and ethnology often argue from a chronological perspective, their studies being made diachronically, while the long chronological perspective is traditionally not that important to sociology and anthropology. Their analyses and arguments are more often synchronic. On the other hand, it is vital for anthropology, sociology as well as for ethnology to ground their argumentation in a cultural and social context, which is not always equally emphasised by historians.

In recent decades, a growing number of books on fashion and dress-related subjects have been published, especially within the social and cultural sciences. Internationally, the focus has been on contemporary fashion and dress cultures in the contemporary consumer society in the West. Books have been written on fashion as a system of signs, fashion as an aspect of communication, clothing as part of material culture, the meaning of dress in identity for individuals and groups, dress and sexuality, and dress and the cultural construction of gender, to mention some of the actual themes.

DIFFERENT TYPES OF MUSEUMS – DIFFERENT TYPES OF DRESS COLLECTIONS

Museums generally work, collect, analyse and exhibit differently. In Denmark, primarily two types of museums collect dress, textiles and costume: design museums and cultural history museums.

The principles of collecting at cultural history museums differ in important ways from the museological praxis at design museums. At art and design museums, art and design – obviously - are at the centre of attention. This implies a certain view on textile, dress and costume. The textile collection at The Danish Museum of Art and Design in Copenhagen features highlights from most areas of textile art. Here more focus is placed on the product (design and form), and the producer (designer). Moreover, high artistic and technical standards are more interesting than, for instance, the use of the design, or the person or groups who have used the dress or textile.

The collections at the cultural history museums are more diverse, and vary due to their specific or regionally defined task, but the general perspective on culture, society and on material objects to include in or exclude from the collections are to some extent similar. Special museums document cultures of specific groups in society, such as military dress (The Royal Danish Arsenal Museum), royal dress (Rosenborg Castle and Amalienborg Museum), or working class dress (The Workers' Museum).

The dress collections at most of the cultural history museums in Denmark contain many different kinds of costumes. The purpose of collecting today is primarily to document the differentiated life of people – groups and individuals – who have lived or live their life or part of it – in Denmark. Dresses, textiles and costumes are interesting for the cultural historic museums from the perspective of production as well as consumption. Dresses in such a collection are not automatically qualified by being of a high artistic or technical standard – although this does not disqualify them either. Cultural history museums of today emphasize dresses and costumes, which can tell stories about culture and conditions of daily life, and it is important that dresses are collected, analysed, explained and understood in a broad cultural, social and historical context. This means that dress collections contain ordinary and well-worn clothes, as well as expensive designer dresses; and that museums document clothes from everyday life as well as special occasions such as weddings and funerals. Cultural history museums – ideally – document what people wear at work and at leisure; they document subcultural dress as, for instance, that of rockers, hip hoppers and hippies; clothes of the young and the old, the thick and the thin. Extensive documentation of the use of the dresses and their users is an important criterion for a cultural historic museum and, often, the museum will try to obtain additional information such as photographic documentation and narratives that may enlighten the life of a new dress in the collection, for instance, as to its use, its user and its producer.

BEHIND THE MUSEUM'S SCENES: TWO CASES OF WORKING WITH 19TH AND 20TH CENTURY HISTORICAL DRESS

Visitors at museums see and experience only the surface of a museum's work. They observe and hear; they taste and smell what the museum staff presents to them for instance at exhibitions, in concerts and other cultural arrangements as well as in the museum café. The visitors are also met with infrastructural remedies such as signs and texts, and they may be offered guidebooks and guided tours.

In this section, we invite the readers into the chambers behind this visible and audible surface of the museum to examine two cases. *Den Gamle By* sets the stage, and thus a short presentation is necessary. *Den Gamle By* – The Old Town – is an open-air museum for Danish urban history and culture situated in Aarhus, the second largest city of Denmark. The collection of more than 75 reconstructed, historical, urban buildings constitutes the core of the museum. However, beyond this, *Den Gamle By* has several special collections of for instance silverware, china and crockery, toys, furniture, clocks, bicycles and, of more relevance to us, a large collection of historical dresses and textiles. Since 1921, this special collection of *Den Gamle By* has been accorded its own section leader, who in 1938 was appointed curator.

In the first case study, we consider the decision-making involved in reconstructing costumes for Living History performances. This line of work has been an integral part of *Den Gamle By* since 2001 (Bloch Ravn 2001, 7–13). In the second case study, we examine the background and decisions for collecting historical dress, in this specific case, wedding clothes from 1950 to 2000. We also discuss the problems of working with contemporary historical sources.

Costumes for Living History performances

In this first case study we look at the close relationship between research and the presentation of experiences with their deliberate sensory appeal to museum visitors, with the aim of furthering the understanding of historical matters. We also discuss the underlying considerations when using sources and show how knowledge is constructed in relation to the project of reconstructing costumes for Living History performances.

In 2001, *Den Gamle By* made 40 costumes in cooperation with the Costume Department of DR, the Danish public service television channel. A thorough documentation of the source material of these costumes was published in the yearbook, *Den Gamle By 2001* (Mathiassen 2001, 14–42). The project fell into a grey zone between theatrical performance and exhibition: between affecting the senses in a number of ways – costumes being one of them – and displaying original items in a showcase. The Living History project was based on historical dates and character performances with certain preconditions with regard to status, gender and age. The roles were chosen in relation to the overall presentation of historical themes from 1840, 1864 and 1885, which was to take place at the museum, and not according to stylistic changes in historical dress over a period of time. It was not possible then to use the original clothes from the museum storerooms as a starting point.

Fig. 9.5: A party among peasants in the Hedebo region *painted by Julius Exner in 1855. Exner collected the material for this painting in the village of Thorslunde, but he painted it in his studio in Copenhagen. The models were young residents of Copenhagen. (Statens Museum for Kunst, Nr. KMS737)*

The work had to be planned in quite another way. The main problem was that the source material – the material objects, the written sources, the paintings and drawings of the different periods – could not answer all questions that arose when living performers in historic dress performed in the streets and houses of *Den Gamle By* (Figs 9.6 –9.7).

For instance, the collection did not own a complete suit for a shoemaker's wife from the year 1840, because the collections had been made by the first two curators from completely different preconditions and collecting principles. The first, Petra Julie Holm, had been in charge of the collection from 1921 to 1959. Thanks to her effort, the collection of historical dress and textiles expanded so much, that in 1939, the dress-collection was given its own building. Her methods were primarily founded on the history of arts and crafts and only

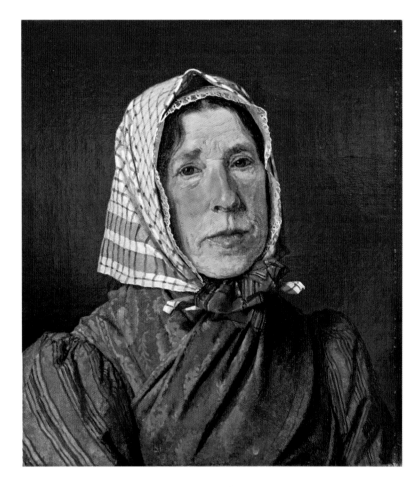

Fig. 9.6: A painting by the Danish artist Christen Købke from 1832 of a peasant woman gives precise information about the taste and combination of items of a bygone era. (Courtesy of Randers Kunstmuseum; Photo: Niels Erik Højrup)

dress and textiles representing the finest and best items had been incorporated in the collections. Holm's successor, Dr. Erna Lorenzen, was in charge of the collection from 1959 to 1979. She attached importance to both giving the collection a broader social scope when acquiring items, and also registering more information about the use of these items, in order to improve the scientific value of the collection (Lorenzen 1975).

The aims of the first curators of the collection were certainly not to collect historical dress in order to make costumes for Living History performances. Their purpose, from their individual points of view and different scientific training, was to create a fine and representative collection of dress and textiles.

Thus, as it was not possible for us in 2001 to pick a complete garment for a shoemaker's wife from the year 1840, a maid from the year 1864, or a housewife from the

Fig. 9.7: The reconstruction of complete outfits from 1840 was among other sources inspired by the work of Christen Købke. (Photo: Henrik Bjerregrav)

year 1885, a whole array of sources were combined and used to obtain the concrete results for the costumes for Living History performances. We used sources such as paintings, drawings, photos, probate estate files, memoirs, clothing and parts of clothing from the collection of *Den Gamle By* (Mathiassen 2001, 14–42). Not every source was equally valid for the work. For instance, as mentioned earlier, certain pictures of 19th century garments had been produced with quite different aims than historical accuracy in terms of cut, materials and colours.

At the end of the 18th century and the beginning of the 19th century, several series of pictures of people's clothing were published all over Europe. There was a general striving towards knowledge – and the pictures had decorative purposes as well. The relatively inexpensive pictures were placed on the inside of chests or framed and placed as decorative items on the walls. These pictures had captions about the origin of the clothing, and they helped form the viewers' ideas of contemporary clothing, and furthermore gave a rigid and uniform concept of clothes to the country. At first, the foreign series were published in Denmark, but soon locally produced series were created. In the period 1854–1861, artist F. C. Lund was paid by the Ministry of Cultural Affairs to travel around Denmark in order to paint and draw peasant costumes for a volume of 30 pictures of *Danish national costumes* (Figs 9.8–9.9). The garments depicted were found at the bottom of people's chests, and parts of the costumes were combined based on aesthetic criteria rather than on any knowledge of their former use or the way the single items had been combined by their original users.

Apart from the paintings and other sources, the collection of historical dress and textiles in *Den Gamle By* was used in the work with the Living History project as well. Historical clothes could give precise information about complete costumes, details of cut, seams and hems, about choice and availability of materials on the market, but they could only sporadically tell us about social strata, taste and preferences of people living in Danish cities in 1840, 1864 and 1885. We thus needed to take a more empathic approach when creating new totalities of clothing. How would for instance the shoemaker's wife in the year 1840 wear her dress, apron, scarf, shawl, shoes and headgear inside and outside the house? What would she choose of the materials in fashion at the time? What could she afford to buy? What was her taste in colours?

We can conclude that the background for working with the costumes for Living History performances was a certain – hopefully significant – amount of knowledge, supplemented by an empathic attitude. When the source material fails, an empathic approach needs to be used. From their very beginnings, this way of proceeding has been integrated in open-air museums. Take for instance, the largest exhibits – the historical buildings. Not every part of a building is kept up in its original state. Changes have been made because people have lived in the house and they have changed it according to their needs and finances. Girders have rotted and have been renewed. Wall painting and the disposition of rooms have been changed according to the taste of different epochs. When a museum chooses to fix a building of a certain date, be it 1768 or 1833, then some parts of the building have to be reconstructed. The building is examined in detail to find the traces, where the building itself tells its story, but the traces have to be interpreted. The museum staff has to make a series of well-founded choices in order to achieve a concrete result. They use the written sources about the building such as craftsmen's bills, fire insurance records, and probate estate files. The work is a creative interaction between written and other sources.

This led to the Danish open-air museums having a kind of pariah status in the museum world from their very foundation, an *enfant terrible* whose mission was to popularize knowledge through a non-scientific, sensory approach. The 'real' museums were scientific in their approach, which at that time meant positivistic. Thus in the early 20th century,

Fig. 9.8: Alexline, the wife of artist F. C. Lund, had to pose in old clothes, when he could not convince young, local girls to pose for him. The sleeves from the beginning of the 1830s may be clearly seen. (Courtesy of Den Gamle By*).*

empathy was not considered an integral part of the scientific process. In the past 100 years, however, views on scientific approaches have changed a great deal and we have realized that the sources cannot answer every question when working with reconstructions of dress or buildings.

Documenting wedding clothes from 1950 to 2000

In this case we can see how the individual curator can influence the quality and substance of the sources for wedding outfits and wedding celebrations for the last 50 years. When a curator collects and documents contemporary historical dress, he or she has a unique opportunity to obtain a source material, which can help answer specific questions about the subject matter.

In 1967, at the marriage of the then Danish Crown Princess, Her Royal Highness Margrethe to the French count Henri de Montpezat, the opportunity was taken by Erna Lorenzen, the then leader of

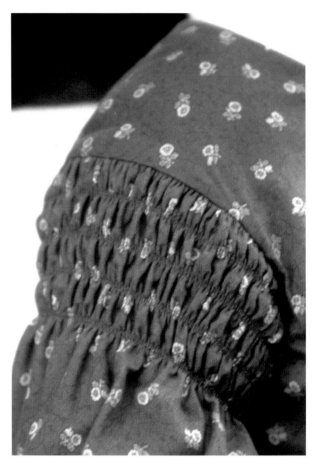

Fig. 9.9: The shoemaker's wife from 1840 had sleeves from the 1830s. However, in contrast to Fig. 9.8, these are from the end of the decade. Detail. (Photo: Henrik Bjerregrav)

the dress-collection in *Den Gamle By*, to establish a collection of wedding clothes with examples from every social stratum. Similarly in 2004, when the Danish Crown Prince, His Royal Highness Frederik married the Australian Mary Donaldson, *Den Gamle By* celebrated the occasion by exhibiting 50 examples of wedding outfits from the last 250 years in the exhibition "Bride and Groom" (Kjær, Mathiassen and Meyer 2004). At the same time, the museum aimed to supply and enlarge the existing collection with examples of wedding clothing from the last 40 years (Mathiassen 2001, 29–33), later extending the scope of the research to the last 50 years, because very interesting examples from the

1950s were offered to the museum. Among the general public, there is a great interest in the subject matter when the royal family celebrates a very common, festive occasion in a royal manner. With the help of the media, the museum could thus get in touch with potential donors of wedding outfits.

We asked ourselves the following questions: What is a good and representative collection of clothing for brides and grooms? What type of information would be useful to obtain in connection with the garments? In other words, how is knowledge produced through an academic approach?

Everyone who donated their wedding clothes to this collection were asked the same questions in an informal manner, aiming at establishing a good and useful source material concerning wedding outfits for men and women in Denmark from the period 1950–2000 (Figs 9.10–9.11). Photos and written documents, songs and speeches, table decorations, and in one case the rings as well, were given to the museum together with the clothes. The enquiries concerned the exact time, place and setting of the wedding, as well as the names and birthdays of bride and groom, and their occupations at the time of the wedding to indicate the social stratum. Other questions concerned the wedding celebrations. Who took part? What were the setting of the celebration, the menu, the entertainment and so forth? Who paid for the expenses? The most important questions were about the clothing, the hairdo and the bouquet – especially concerning the types of aesthetic choices that were made for the festive occasion. Why did the bride or the groom wish to present themselves exactly like this? Very interesting

Fig. 9.10: This bride from 1954 was inspired by American fashion magazines when she had to decide on the style of her wedding dress. (Courtesy of Den Gamle By)

comments and considerations followed the clothes into the museum. The large number of questions posed gave the donors an opportunity to tell yet other stories about the celebration or the clothing. This large source material is still being examined with publication in mind.

CONCLUSIONS

There is a vast bulk of sources of various types, when we work with historical dress from modern Danish history. The clothes themselves are important sources of information, especially when combined with written and pictorial evidence of many types; they offer an image of the period and social strata in question. Furthermore, several academic disciplines, be it art history, social anthropology, ethnology, sociology or history, view historical dress from their different perspectives. The results of the different approaches are different in that the methods have consequences for the research. One of the cases of museum work examined shows how having a chance to collect dresses of modern times gives the researcher an opportunity to work consciously

Fig. 9.11: In 1988, this couple arranged their wedding with a Prince and Princess party as a theme. The dress was made by the Danish fashion designer Maria Sander, and the bouquet from a specialist flower arranger, Tage Andersen. Each detail of the wedding had to reflect the theme. (Courtesy of Den Gamle By)

with the production of knowledge while documenting.

When designers or design schools work with historical dress, it is important to be critical about their own methods. When working with the precise reconstruction of dress we must be critical and conscious in the search for, and the use of, sources. We should be aware of gender, class and potential taste, when, for instance, the task is to reconstruct the garment of a shoemaker's wife in its entirety. Yet, it is still important to realize that at the same time the past is a legitimate treasure chest of inspiration for artistic work. Designers can use any detail or totality from a historic dress as inspiration for any design in the present. However, this line of work does not constitute reconstruction, but rather creative work on the basis of historical sources, which is quite another matter.

BIBLIOGRAPHY

In this chapter, the following works have been used:

Andersen, E. (1960) *Danske bønders klædedragt.* Copenhagen, Carit Andersen.

Andersen, E. (1977) *Moden i 1700-årene.* Copenhagen, Nationalmuseet.

Bloch Ravn, T. (2001) Levende Museum. In the Yearbook, *Den Gamle By, Aarhus.* Århus, Den Gamle By, 7–13.

Kjær, B., T. Engelhardt Mathiassen and F. Meyer (eds) (2004) *Brud og brudgom*, Den Gamle Bys skriftrække VIII. Århus, Den Gamle By.

Lorenzen, E. (1975) *Folks tøj i og omkring Aarhus ca. 1675– ca. 1850.* Jysk Selskab for Historie. Århus, Universitetsforlaget.

Lorenzen, E. (1987) *Hvem sagde Nationaldragt?* Højbjerg, Worminanum.

Mathiassen, T. Engelhardt (2001) En halv kilometer stof – eller hvordan et museum arbejder med dragter. In the Yearbook, *Den Gamle By, Aarhus.* Århus, Den Gamle By, 14–42.

Zenius, M. (1976) *Genremaleri og virkelighed.* Skrifter udgivet af Lokalhistorisk afdeling, no. 6, Copenhagen.

Readers are further recommended to consult the following websites:

www.dragt.dk This has an English version. Here it is also possible to find museum collections containing dress and textiles from all over Denmark. The National Museum of Denmark in Copenhagen and the Open Air Museum *Den Gamle by* (The Old Town) in Århus contain the two largest cultural historic dress and textile collections in the country.

www.natmus.dk

www.dengamleby.dk

www.kunstindustrimuseet.dk

www.dmol.dk

www.kid.dk

Chapter 10

Cut, Stitch and Fabrics: Female Dress in the Past 200 Years

Maj Ringgaard

Fabrics, their cut and designs change over time. Knowing where to place seams, darts, openings and which type of fastener to use helps to create the right shape and look when copying costumes from paintings, photographs and other visual images. This chapter presents examples of how the mounting and placing of the opening of a dress changed in the course of the 19th and early 20th century, with the main focus on the 19th century. It examines where and when hooks and loops, buttons, zippers, padding and boning were used, where the side seams, gores and darts were placed, and which fabrics were preferred in costumes of this period. Equally important, when examining a historical dress, knowing these details can help you date it correctly.

Keywords: fashion, sewing machine, sewing techniques, stitching, fabric, fastenings, historical dress, tailoring.

Creating the right historic costumes for a film or a play is often a balance between costs, time and opportunity. A splendid illusion can be brutally spoiled in a moment when a glance at the back of a young Victorian woman reveals a zipper in her dress. On the other hand, neat little details like a special lacing or the right kind of garter on the heroine's thigh makes the experience of looking at a historic scene even better, as for example in the opening scene of the movie *Dangerous Liaisons*, where actress Glenn Close is dressed by her servants and the dress is closed by stitching. Details like these make the film appealing even to the connoisseur.

DRESS: DESIGN AND MATERIALS

The typical female dress of the 18th century consisted of a dress open at the front with a petticoat or skirt. This type of open dress, the *mantua*, made the front part of the skirt visible. The gap at the front from the waist upwards was covered by a stomacher, a stiff triangular piece of stiffened fabric, sometimes, but not always, matching the dress. The stomacher was often highly decorated with gold or silk embroidery and laces (Andersen 1977). The dress materials were heavy crisp silks with woven flower-patterns, which gave the dress a stiff appearance. Servants and commoners wore a short jacket made of printed linen or wool damask and a woollen. The dresses were fully lined with linen (Fig. 10.1).

Dress from the 1790s was of the chemise type with a high waist; the Empire period dress was based on the classical Greek ideal. The materials were gauzelike fabrics of linen,

Fig. 10.1: Woman's dress. (Diderot's Encyclopaedia *1763)*

nettle, ramie, or cotton; muslin was predominantly white, often with a printed pattern in lilac. Ten years later, the waistline was at its highest, placed right under the bust. The bodice and sleeves were sometimes unlined, or lined with plain white linen or muslin. Long sleeves had a short inner sleeve instead of lining. The dress was open at the front. The front of the bodice consisted of two parts, each with a plain inner layer and a gathered outer layer. The plain inner parts were fastened with hooks and eyes or simply pinned under the breast and acted like a brassiere. The outer parts were gathered, giving fullness to the breast as seen on Fig. 10.3. The dress was fastened with fine draw-strings made of linen thread or very narrow tapes. The back of the bodice was diamond shaped and narrow, with the armholes set very much to the back. The skirt had an 'apron front', being only stitched to the bodice at the back. The skirt front was fastened with ribbon ties or bindings or pinned at the sides. The skirt had a train or was just slightly longer at the back than the front (Figs 10.2–10.3).

Twenty years later, it became more common to have dresses with back openings

Fig. 10.2: Dress dated 1798, white muslin with multicoloured silk embroidery at the hem. The short sleeves, side parts and the diamond shaped centre back are decorated with pin tucks. The armholes are cut deep at the back. The front parts are double layered and fastened at the diamond shaped back. The gathered skirt is 48 cm longer at the back creating a train. (National Museum of Denmark no. 427/1923; Photo: Roberto Fortuna)

Fig. 10.3: Front of dress shown in Fig. 10.2. The skirt is only fastened to the bodice at the back; the 'apron front' has no fastening and must have been pinned at the sides. The dress is unlined but the front parts are double, the under parts are quite narrow and plain and were pinned or stitched under the bust, the outer parts are gathered and are fastened with drawstrings through the hems over and under the bust. (National Museum of Denmark no. 427/1923; Photo: Roberto Fortuna)

rather than front openings. The floor-length skirt was fully joined to the bodice. Seams on the back of the bodice were often piped. The short waist level jacket, called a spencer, worn together with muslin dresses, was often dark in colour: green, blue or black, of woollen fabric, sometimes with a woven or printed pattern. Spencers were fully lined with fine linen or plain-woven silk fabric.

During the 1820–1830s, the waistline was lowered until it reached the natural waist level. More colours were used, with fabrics often made of printed cotton, calico, or silk. The bodice and sleeves were fully lined with plain linen or cotton weave. In puffed sleeves, the lining was not puffed. The shoulders were lowered so the sleeves started on the upper part of the arm. Seams on the bodice were all piped. The bodice was boned at mid-back. Skirt hems were corded, padded or filled with rows of frills to give volume to the skirt at the hem. At the waist, skirts were only gathered at the back, but plain in front, and were gored in order to obtain the required fullness at the hem (Figs 10.4–10.6).

Around 1850, the dress was open in front, fastened with small buttons or hooks and eyes. Hooks and eyes were often placed alternately to prevent them from opening when moving. Dress was now two-pieced, with skirt and bodice separate. The bodice was often opened in front with small buttons or hooks and eyes. A skirt often had two different bodices, one for daytime wear and another with a low neck-line and back opening, some-times closed with lacing for evening wear . The bodice was fitted with darts, and the bust rounded.

The skirts were wide and stiffened with several petti-coats. At the end of the 1850s, some of the petticoats were substituted by a 'cage' of steel bands: the crinoline. The skirt was open at the side and a pocket was often placed in a

Fig. 10.4: A blue and beige silk dress from about 1845. The pointed front of the bodice made the waist look slim, and is typical for the mid-19th century. Bodice and skirt are fully attached; the dress opens at the back. There are piped seams on shoulders and armholes. (National Museum of Denmark no. 725/1948; Photo: Roberto Fortuna)

side seam of the skirt. The fabrics were heavier silks and woollens, often in blue, green, dark brown and mauve. Then, in the 1860s, the crinoline was flattened at the front, giving the impression of a woman standing in one end of an ellipse. The skirts had flounces, often with decorations.

In the 1870s, the princess silhouette became fashionable. This was a panelled-cut, one-

Fig. 10.5: The inside of the silk dress shown in Fig. 10.4. The dress is fully lined, the bodice with calendered linen, the sleeves and skirt with lightweight cotton. The bodice is boned with 18 thin whalebones sewn onto the reverse side of the lining; the canals for the bones are seen as fine hand-stitched lines. The ends of the bones are secured with a fan-shaped bunch of stitches. The sleeves with lining are sewn onto the armhole in one go; here and at the back of the waist are the only places where the edges are visible. The edges are finished with an overcast seam. The bodice is fastened with hooks; instead of eyes, small eyelets are sewn. Inserted in the side seam of the skirt is a pocket made of yellow chintz, between the waist and the pocket is a linen tape attached to prevent the pocket from tearing the silk fabric. (National Museum of Denmark, no. 725/1948; Photo: Roberto Fortuna)

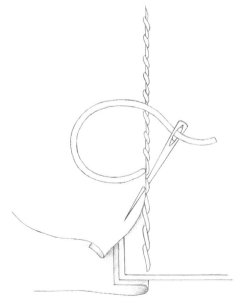

Fig. 10.6: The blue silk face fabric and the white linen lining were sewn in two steps as shown in this drawing. (Courtesy of K. Toftegaard)

Fig. 10.7: Jacket-like bodice from the late 1870s. The jacket is of a rustic home-made type, but the cut follows the fashion with the longer waist and the buttoned front opening and sleeves with two seams. The pattern is probably from one of the newly popular women's magazines. The back is cut in one part but has a center back seam, perhaps an alteration to make a slimmer fit. The seams at the armholes are reinforced with piping. The shoulder and the side seams are set towards the back. The face fabric is of home woven linsey-woolsey, striped in brown, pale blue and purple. This purple colour, mauve, is one of the first synthetic colours and became very popular in the 1870s. The waist, neck and cuffs are made of dark brown cotton velvet. This shows how the fashion was adapted by common people: the cut follows the fashion, but the materials are less expensive or home-made.

Around the neck was usually a thin white collar. Instead of the lace-collar used by the higher echelons of society, this dress had probably a knitted or crocheted collar of white cotton yarn. (The Open Air Museum, National Museum of Denmark, no. 49.604; Photo: Roberto Fortuna)

piece dress with long straight lines and no waist seam, gathered at the back and draped over a bustle or a half crinoline with no steel ribs in front. The dress was often open at the front, fastened with ball-shaped fabric-covered buttons. At the waistline, there was often a waistband that could be fastened before doing the outer fasteners, helping the bodice to

Fig. 10.8: The lining of the jacket illustrated in Fig. 10.7 is of two different types of plain woven linen, the coarser one being hand woven. The seams are made with the face fabric and the lining together and stitched with only one seam so the raw edges are visible inside the bodice. By this time the sewing machine was widely used, but in this jacket all seams are hand stitched. The side seams are altered and stitched with a coarser thread. At the waist is a horizontal dart between the second front dart and the side seam, this gives a better fit and prevents folds on the sides. The bodice has neither boning nor a waistband. Compared to the dress in Fig. 10.5 or the bodice in Fig. 10.10, it is obvious that this jacket has been made by an amateur.

Hooks inside at the centre back are for fastening to corresponding eyes on the skirt, thus taking the weight of the skirt from the waist. There is a strap inside each of the shoulders for hanging the bodice on a peg. (The Open Air Museum, National Museum of Denmark, no. 49.604; Photo: Roberto Fortuna)

stay in place and preventing it from creeping upwards. The waistband also relieved stress on the tight fitting garment and made it easier to open and close it. The ideal bust was a smooth, rounded shape. This effect could be obtained with a padded filling in the hollow between bust and armhole, and on the chest over the bust. Soft silk covered pads were either sewn on, or inserted into the dress (Tarrant 1996, 117) (Figs 10.9–10.10).

Dress in the 1890s often looked one-piece, but in fact was always two-pieced. The bodice often had complicated cuts and fastenings, like, for instance, a bodice that gave the impression of two or three garments in different materials layered on top of each other. The different parts of the bodice are mounted on the lining which still had a simple slim fitting shape. Fastenings used were hooks and eyes, tinier than those used earlier in the century, as well as small buttons. The buttons were often only for decoration, the fastening

Fig. 10.9: Black silk bodice with black glass-bead decorations, sleeves with tiny velvet bands and black silk lace, about 1890. (The Open Air Museum, National Museum of Denmark; Photo: Roberto Fortuna)

being press studs under the buttons. Press studs were also used for fastening decorative elements like lace collars (Fig. 10.9).

The bodice became increasingly fuller and, by the turn of the century, the front fell over the waist; this, together with the skirt's flat front, fullness at the back and a little train at the back, gave the woman an S-shaped figure (Cock-Clausen 1994, 86). Skirts were opened near the centre back, and a pocket was often placed in the opening seam.

After 1900, the waist was accentuated by a belt; both belt and waistline gradually moved upwards so that by the beginning of the 1910s, the high Empire-style waistline was back. The dress resembled a pinafore with a blouse underneath, but the effect was in fact obtained by using lighter fabric in the sleeves and as a vest. This pinafore dress was often made of dark-coloured woollen fabrics with sleeves and vest in white or light coloured muslin, tulle or lace. These garments often had a concealed opening: the bodice of the dress had an inner lining in the shape of a tight fitting bodice on which the dress was

Fig. 10.10: View of inside of bodice in Fig. 10.9. This well-tailored bodice has the name of the dressmaker stamped on the waistband. The lining is of printed satin woven cotton fabric, one pattern in the bodice and another in the sleeves. There are twelve body pieces. At the seams the lining and the face fabric are treated as one fabric, indicating that the seams were made in one go. Seam allowances are pressed apart and cut in rounds before being neatened to give room for the tight-fitting curves. Fifteen steel bones are covered with tubes of the lining fabric and placed on the major body seams; the bones in the sides and the front are covered with black ribbon. Dress protectors of white cotton help maintain a clean and tidy appearance. Straps are placed at the back of the arm seam for hanging the bodice. (The Open Air Museum, National Museum of Denmark; Photo: Roberto Fortuna)

draped, similar to the bodice linings of previous decades. This lining was opened either at the back or front, while the draped dress was opened at the side, or where the opening could be hidden in the drapes. The lining was closed with hooks and eyes, while the dress was fastened with press studs. A dressmaking and sewing instruction book from the late 1910s mentions that the lining should always be made first and the adjustments completed before the outer layers are made. Then, four pages of how to sew and adjust the lining follows (Anon *c.* 1918, 38–42).

After the First World War, the cut changed to a much simpler shift-cut style skirt and bodice in one: one back and one front piece, with one-seam sleeves. Even the opening disappeared; the dress was put on by simply pulling it down over the head.

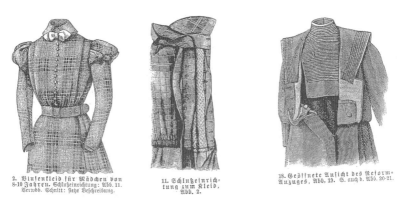

Fig. 10.11: These drawings from the German women's magazine Die Modenwelt *(1898) show double opening systems with hidden hooks and eyes under a buttoned front; these are typical for a dress from the end of the 19th century.*

Fig. 10.12: Bodice of grey mohair made by a dressmaker in 1911. The bodice gives the impression of a jacket on top of a high-necked blouse of the same material. The body is lined with yellow cotton damask, the sleeves with grey satin-woven cotton. (National Museum of Denmark no. 996/1937; Photo: Roberto Fortuna)

Fig. 10.13: The lining of the bodice in Fig. 10.12 shows a bodice in eight body pieces. Here the front and back parts are lined separately, so the seam allowance is only seen in the side seams. The boning is placed in hollows made in the lining seams, the boning made of flat steel spirals is held in place by star shaped stitching with thick yellow thread. The hooks on the back of the waistband correspond with eyes on the skirt. The bodice is fastened with eyes on the left and hooks on the right front piece; the lining is fastened with alternating hooks and eyes. The belt is fastened with press studs. Over the bust is a grey, printed cotton-covered padding between the face fabric and the lining. (National Museum of Denmark no. 996/ 1937; Photo: Roberto Fortuna)

Around 1920, the dress began to resemble a loose-fitting shift. The tight fitting inner bodice was exchanged for an inner slip, open at the side, on which the dress was mounted. The preferred materials were silk, crêpe-de-Chine, georgette or lace.

BONING

In the first half of the 19th century, boning was made of whalebone, split willow, cane or even wooden sticks. The boning was inserted into the seam in a casing made of the lining. In the second half of 19th century, the bones were made of flexible bands of steel with rounded ends and small eyes for fastenings, and at the end of the century – of flattened spirals of steel. The steel bones had an eye at both ends which could be fastened by stitching, often in the shape of a half star. The steel bones were inserted into the seams or stitched onto the seams with bands holding them in place; by the end of the 19th century, these bands were tubular-woven.

The earlier types of bones had been very stiff and were often fewer than in the later more flexible types. In the 1830s, the typical bodice had two or four bones; while in 1890, the number had increased to 11 or 13 (Fig. 10.14). Boning in dress stopped after the First World War, but became fashionable again in the 1950s in evening dresses. Now, however, the boning was made of flexible nylon.

CUT

The way garments were cut and sewn shows two different traditions: homemade underwear on the one hand, and tailor-made outer garments on the other. The silhouette or shape of the former was created by folds and gathers, instead of darts and shape-cut parts.

Underwear shifts and men's shirts were based on only square and triangular pieces. The fabric had as few cuts as possible. These garments went back to a time when the approach to fabric was almost sacred and nothing was discarded.

Outer garments like dresses, jackets and trousers were made by tailors or dressmakers. The cut of these garments was more elaborate. A bodice was made of many parts cut into forms, to fit the body and create the required silhouette: two or four front pieces, two side pieces and one centre back piece.

Around 1800, the chemise type of sewing techniques, formerly used in underwear, began now to be used in dressmaking (Hammar and Rasmussen 2001, 128), but the bodice and sleeves were still cut into shapes, following the tradition of the outer garments.

The main parts for a dress bodice consisted of these five to nine shaped bodice parts, one or two-pieced sleeves and a skirt, until the late 1910s, when the simple shift-cut, later popular in the 1920s, was introduced. The couturier, Paul Poiret, re-invented the simple T-shaped dress and tunic in 1906, leaving out the boning in dress. His ideas of a simple cut dress spread slowly during the 1910s (Ginsburg 1975, 11).

From the 18th century and until about 1900, the shoulder seams were set towards the back; this and the back part being smaller than today forced the shoulders backwards creating a straighter back for the wearer than is usual today (Figs 10.15, 10.16, 10.17).

Patterns were distributed by women's magazines, published in many European

Fig. 10.14: In this short silk jacket, the boning is held in place between two pockets in the fabric lining so the whalebone is visible. This made it possible to use the same bones in other garments. This method of fastening the boning is never used in professional dress-making and shows that the jacket probably belonged to a country-woman who made it herself. The linen lining is not attached to the face fabric on the right front but is fastened with hooks and eyes. Note how the eyes are placed in a fold held in place with a fine row of backstitching so only the very tops of the eyes are visible. The black silk face fabric is fastened with silk home-made buttons. (National Museum of Denmark no. 459/1922; Photo: Roberto Fortuna)

countries; the patterns and illustrations often appeared in many different magazines with the text adapted to the country. In Germany, for instance *Die Modenwelt* and *Bazar* appeared, while in Denmark *Dagmar* and *Nordisk Mønstertidende* were published.

Fashionable women in the cities could see the latest magazine at their dressmaker or bring their own fabric and fashion magazine from which they could chose a pattern and discuss details with the dressmaker. The same magazine pattern would be used by several women. Perhaps a maid would inherit it and bring it back to the village where other women could use it. In this way, fashion spread and was adapted by common people.

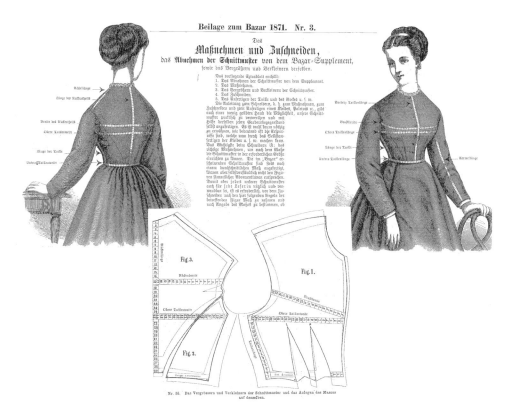

Fig. 10.15: Directions for how to create a pattern from body measurements and for sewing, from the German women's magazine Bazar *(1871). It is a typical pattern for the waist-length bodices of the 1860s and beginning of the 1870s. The bodice is made of one centre back piece, two side back pieces and two front pieces. The front pieces each have two darts to give fullness to the bust. The shoulder seams are set towards the back. The ideal was to have slanted shoulders accentuated with a low shoulder-line. The sleeves are one seam.*

Among them, the cut of the garment would resemble fashionable dress, but the materials used were less expensive and the finish different. Often, home woven fabric and other homemade materials such as bands, braids and crocheted edgings were used, as may be seen in the jacket in Figs 10.7 and 10.8 (Tarrant 1996, 128; Hammar and Rasmussen 2001, 63; Cock-Clausen 1994, 184).

At the beginning of the 19th century, fullness at the bust was given by gathering. By the mid-century, it was created by two darts at each side of the front. This was the most popular style until it changed completely after the First World War. In the 1920s, dress was loose and not form-fitting, with extra width to the bust due to inserted parts, sometimes on the slant. In the 1930s, the width was given by shoulder darts, which were

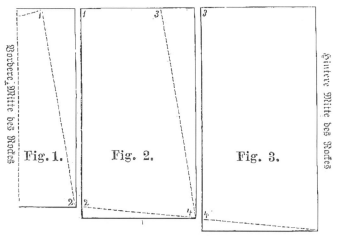

Nr. 56. Anleitung zum Zuschneiden eines Rockes.

Fig. 10.16: The ellipse-shaped crinolines with a flat front and skirts fuller at the back than front were created by increasing the length at the back and by adding a piece with straight grain direction to a bias cut, as seen on this cutting pattern from Bazar *1871. This skirt is made from 5 parts, with each a whole fabric width; for an evening dress, one or two extra parts or fabric widths could be added. A pocket was often inserted in the seam between the front and side panel.*

substituted by gathering in the 1940s. With the 'new look' after the Second World War, the look of the mid-19th century was back: slim waist, dropping shoulders and wide skirts. Now, the fullness of the bust was due to upward pointing darts from the waist and the side seam. Then, in the 1960s, the darts moved over the bust starting from the armholes (Fig. 10.18).

From 1920 to about 1960, lingerie strap holders were placed on strategic places in the dress to secure underwear straps, as it was not thought appropriate for underwear straps to be seen. In the 1930s, the deep back cut on evening dress required several of these straps to be placed along the neckline.

STITCHING

All seams were hand stitched until the invention of the sewing machine. It is amazing to see how fine the stitching was (see Aneer in this volume). The stitches were often smaller than the finest machine stitching. In the long seams of the skirts, longer stitches and coarser thread were sometimes used. To make the stitching of longer seams easier and faster, the material was fastened to a weighted cushion. Machine stitched seams from the end of the 19th century have much finer, shorter stitches than from the 20th century.

KLÆDER 111

Normalmaal for Længdemaalene.

c, $^1/_1$ Livlængde $=$ 40 cm.
d, $^1/_1$ Sidelængde $=$ 21 cm.

Tag et Stykke Papir **60 cm**. i □. Tegn en Vinkellinje foroven og langs venstre Sidekant af Papiret og mærk Linjernes Skæringspunkt Punkt I.

Længdemaal.*

Maal fra 1—2 $= {}^1/_{12}$ af $^1/_2$ Overvidde $\big\{$ Naar $^1/_1$ Overvidde maaler under 96 cm., lægges $^1/_2$ cm. til Maalene **1-2** og **2-3a**.
Maal - 2—3$_a = {}^1/_{12}$ af $^1/_2$ Overvidde
Maal - 3—4 $= {}^1/_4$ af $^1/_2$ Overvidde $\div$ 1 cm.

Fig. I.

Fig. II

Fig. III.

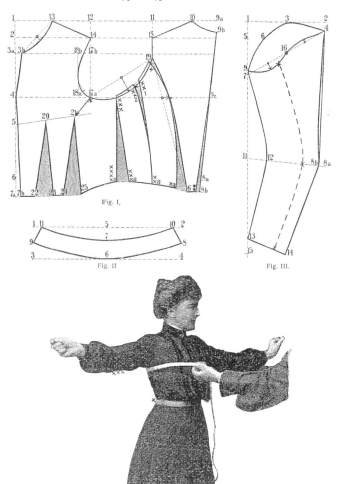

Fig. 10.17: At the end of the 19th century, the bodice was made of several long, shaped parts. The centre back part is divided to give a tighter fitting; the front parts could be divided in two parts instead of darts. The shoulder seams are on top of the shoulders and the sleeves are tight-fitting two-seam sleeves. (After Heckscher 1906, fig. 71, 111)

Perhaps this reflects the tradition of tiny stitches used in hand-stitching throughout the 18th and 19th centuries, which was transferred into the early machine stitching.

The first sewing machine was made by Bartholomé Thimonier in 1829. It used a one thread system making chain stitch. Several improvements followed, and in 1860, Singer developed the two thread system (plain stitch) machine, as it is known today (Waldén 1983). This new technology spread quickly, and soon, it was in common use in dress-making, especially for the long seams in skirts. The use of machine stitching led to more elaborate dresses. The fashion was for many seams and details, for example skirts with three flounces, often with decorations sewn on them. Bodice and skirts were made separately before being joined by hand stitching. The fullness of the skirt was achieved by gathering small pleats held in place by a seam about 2 cm from the edge (Fig. 10.19).

Fig. 10.18: Green rayon-repp blouse, 1952. The tight fitting blouse is pulled over the head; an opening with a zip allows this. The fullness at the bust is given by two darts from the side and one from the waist. (The Open Air Museum, National Museum of Denmark; Photo: Roberto Fortuna)

By the 1880s, the sewing machine had become quite small and inexpensive, making it possible for middle class women to work as dressmakers. Now it was not only the women in the highest levels of society, who could afford to have details on garments that required much stitching, such as flounces, ruching, decorations made of braids and bows made of the dress materials.

After the First World War, as dress became simpler in cut, dress-making became more common at home. Edges were neatened by hand. In the 1920s with its thin fabrics, edges were neatened with a tiny fold held in place by a machine seam. This form of neatening was widely used (if the fabric was not too heavy) until the machines could do zigzag

stitching. The first sewing machine with
zigzag stitching came on the market in the
mid-1940s, but they were not 'every
woman's' until about 1960 (Waldén 1983).
From the 1960s, the overlock sewing
machine was used in industry. This was
time saving as the seams and neatening
were made in one process. Around 1970,
some types of overlock stitching were
introduced on the household sewing
machines. As jersey and stretch materials
became more fashionable, there came a
need for flexible seams in household
sewing machines for mending and
repairing, as well as for home dress-making
(Fig. 10.20).

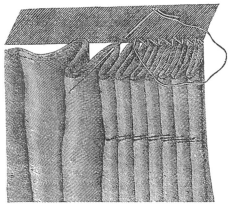

Nr. 63.   Das Arrangement der Queuefalten
und das Annähen derselben an den Gurt.

Fig. 10.19: Drawing from Bazar *(1871),
showing how to arrange and stitch the pleating
while joining a skirt and bodice. In the first half
of the 19th century, the skirt was stitched like
this onto the bodice; in the second half, when
dress and bodice became separate, the skirt was
pleated onto a band.*

LINING

Before 1850, the bodice was lined with
simple linen fabric of different qualities,
with the sleeves often having finer fabric.
Most of the seams and the cut edges were hidden in the lining. Seams were not neatened
because the lining protected them from fraying. The lining, unlike today, was not made as
a separate garment sewn together with the garment, but was more like an underlining
doubling the face fabric, that is the outer fabric. Often, the longer seams of the lining and
the face fabric were sewn in one go. The two parts of the face fabric were put face to face,
as was the lining fabric, and the four layers were placed on top of each other and stitched
together, after which the face fabric was pulled inside out (Fig. 10.21).

Sleeves were often sewn onto the bodice with only one seam; here, the edges from the
bodice and sleeve fabrics and linings were overcast in one go.

After about 1850, lining and face fabric were more or less treated as one fabric. The cut
edges were visible inside the bodice, the seam allowances from both pieces were folded on
one side and the cut edge overcast. If the seams were machine sewn, the edges were
always neatened by hand. Clothes made by a professional dressmaker were often lined
with silk fabrics, and the dressmaker's name could be stamped in the waistband.

Lined skirts had linings of lighter weight, plain linen or cotton fabrics, usually the hem
being lined with a 15–20 cm lining. In simpler home-made clothes, this lining was often
made of several different fabric remnants. The edge of the hem was finished with a braid
sewn over the fabric edge to protect it from wear. At the end of the 19th century, braid
was usually a brush-braid, a woollen band with a woven pile at the edge. The hem edge

could thus be brushed when the dirt was dry (Fig. 10.22).

From about 1870 onwards, the seam allowances were folded on each side of the seam, and both sides overcast. In curved seams, darts were cut in the seam allowance to prevent the seams from bulking. The dress could be lined with different fabrics, with one type in the sleeves, another in the bodice and a third in the skirt. The fabrics were often satin-woven printed cotton, as may be seen in the bodice in Fig. 10.10.

At the end of the 19th century, more elaborated dress designs became fashionable. The bodice was often constructed of a simple bodice-form made of the lining, sometimes supported by a plain-weave cotton fabric, on which the different parts of the bodice were draped.

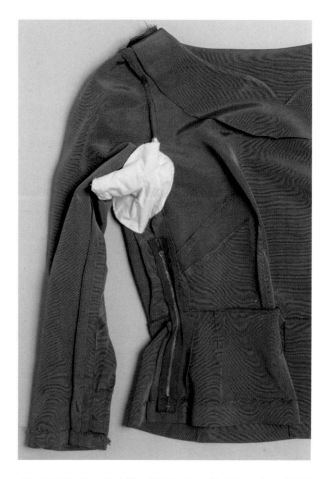

Fig. 10.20: Detail of Fig. 10.18. On this blouse from 1952, the seams are neatened with a tiny fold held in place by a machine seam. The seams around the armhole and at the waist, where the stress is bigger, are neatened with machine zigzag stitching. At the hem, herringbone stitching is used. Hems were not machine stitched until 'invisible machine stitching' was invented in the 1960s. The zip is stitched by hand. (The Open Air Museum, National Museum of Denmark; Photo: Roberto Fortuna)

CONCLUSIONS

In the period discussed, the cut, stitch and fabrics changed several times. Some of the changes were due to new inventions, or technological improvements. Others were just a whim of fashion, expressing the feminine ideal of the period.

A dramatic development in female dress can be seen from the 18th century's stiff, big skirted *mantua* in crisp silk, through the soft high-waisted muslin dress of around 1800, back to the increasingly larger skirts in heavy fabrics, culminating in the big crinolines and

narrow waists in 1860. The
fullness of the skirts was kept,
but the shape was changed by
the use of different kinds of
crinolines, half crinolines and
bustles underneath, and by
gathering, pulling up and
draping the skirts. With the
advent of the sewing machine,
it became possible and practical
to make the highly elaborated
decorations on the dress, bows,
ruffs, flounces all over the skirt
and bodice. The narrow waist
formed with corsets was kept
until about 1910 when the
softer look with a higher waistline was back again, this time in
woollen fabrics for daywear,
and soft silks like georgette,
Japonette or crepe for evening-
wear.

The new artificial silk, rayon
and cellulose acetate, made soft
silk-like dresses and stockings a
part of nearly every woman's
wardrobe, thus making it

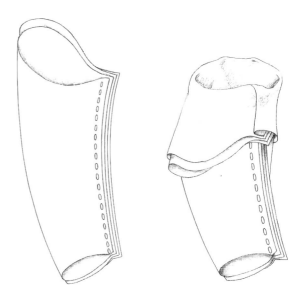

Fig. 10.21: Before the invention of the sewing machine, long seams were very time-consuming, and in order to overcome this, lining and face fabric could be sewn in one go as shown in these drawings. The two parts of the face fabric are placed face to face and the same with the lining fabric, the four layers are put on top of each other and are stitched together after which the face fabric is pulled inside out. (Illustration by Kirsten Toftegaard)

possible to expose the legs in sheer stockings when the skirt length rose in the 1920s. The development of new synthetic colours and new printing techniques prepared the way for colourful patterned fabrics. The simple cut of the 1920s suited the new material and the use of bias-cut in the 1930s accentuated the soft materials. After the Second World War, new synthetic materials came on the market. These easily manageable drip and dry fabrics were perfect for the modern working woman. The first synthetic fibres were hard to dye and were only available in pastel shades, but during the 1960s, new methods and dyes were invented. The synthetic filaments were still not as soft and flexible as natural fibres: the simple A-shape fashion was perfect for these bright multi-coloured fabrics. The later invention of Lycra has had a great influence on fashion, making it possible to move freely in tight-fitting garments.

In every period, certain looks accentuated the feminine ideal of the time, for instance the large skirts, the slim waist and slanted shoulders of the mid-19th century showing the woman as an unapproachable, fragile creature; or the padded-shouldered mannish woman

Fig. 10.22: Lining of the hem of the blue dress shown in Fig. 10.4. The skirt is lined with lightweight cotton; the hem has a 15 cm lining of yellow chintz and is finished with a blue woollen braid. (National Museum of Denmark no. 725/1948; Photo: Roberto Fortuna)

of the 1940s. Each silhouette was the result of a certain combination of cut and material. Thus, using a different fabric would create another look, as would changes in the cut.

Often, a certain fashion experiences a revival several years later, like the slim waist, corsets and wide skirts held out by several petticoats in the 1750s, 1850s and 1950s (see Figs 10.15 and 10.18); or the high waist-line and straight lined skirts without corsets and petticoats in the 1800s, 1910s (introduced by Paul Poiret) and in the late 1960s. Yet, each time a fashion is revived, details in cut, stitch and fabrics are different; it may look the same from a distance, but a closer look reveals its date (Fig. 10.23).

The development of female dress is often considered a reflection of technological changes and of the volatile nature of fashion. However, it was my aim in this chapter to demonstrate that it is such precise details as cut, stitch and linings that form the very basis of female dress and enable the fashion to change. Secondly, it should not be forgotten that cut, stitch and lining, the handicraft of dressmaking, are still extremely time-consuming despite new inventions. Finally, dressmaking requires skills and experience, which technological inventions have not diminished.

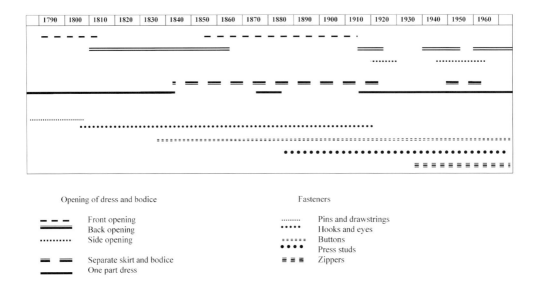

| 1790 | 1800 | 1810 | 1820 | 1830 | 1840 | 1850 | 1860 | 1870 | 1880 | 1890 | 1900 | 1910 | 1920 | 1930 | 1940 | 1950 | 1960 | |

Opening of dress and bodice

- - -   Front opening
═══   Back opening
·········   Side opening

⚌ ⚌   Separate skirt and bodice
▬▬▬   One part dress

Fasteners

·········   Pins and drawstrings
•••••   Hooks and eyes
======   Buttons
••••   Press studs
≡ ≡ ≡   Zippers

Fig. 10.23: Table 1. Timeline of cut and fastening techniques in female dress (1790–1960). (© Maj Ringgaard)

ACKNOWLEDGEMENTS

I would like to thank Kirsten Toftegaard, Curator of the Textile Collection at the Danish Museum of Art and Design for her illustrations (Fig. 10.6 and Fig. 10.21), which were earlier published in *Kvinlig mode under två sekel* by B. Hammar and P. Rasmussen (Lund Signum, 2001).

BIBLIOGRAPHY

General works on the topic are Anon (*c.* 1918) *Sybogen II del Kjolesyning*. Copenhagen, Marius Hartz. (A Danish version of the dressmaking instructions by Butterick Publishing Co., New York, Paris & London); Ginsburg, M. B. (1975) Fashion: an art 1900–1939. In *Fashion 1900–1939*. London, Idea Books International, 10–21; Hammar, B. and P. Rasmussen (2001) *Kvinlig mode under två sekel*. Lund, Signum; Heckscher, D. (1906) Klæder. In Anon, *Haandværk i Hjemmet*, Copenhagen, Frem Nordisk Forlag, 60–133; Tarrant, N. (1996) The art of construction. In *The Development of Costume*. Edinburgh, National Museum of Scotland, 104–135; Waldén, L. *et al.* (1983) *Josefin och teknologin: tekniken sedd genom symaskinens nålsöga*. Stockholm, Sveriges Tekniska Museum.
    Description of dress fashion in Denmark in the 18th and 19th centuries with patterns of some of the garments in the collections of the National Museum of Denmark can be found in

Andersen, E. (1977) *Danske Dragter. Moden i 1700-årene.* Copenhagen, Nationalmuseet; (1986) *Danske Dragter. Moden 1790–1840.* Copenhagen, Nationalmuseet; Bech, V. (1989) *Danske Dragter. Moden 1840–1890.* Copenhagen, Nationalmuseet; Cock-Clausen, I. (1994) *Danske Dragter. Moden 1890–1920.* Copenhagen, Nationalmuseet.

Detailed patterns and drawings of construction details of historical costumes can be found in Arnold, J. (1964) *Patterns of Fashion: Englishwomen's Dresses and their Construction c. 1660–1860.* London, Macmillan; (1966) *Patterns of Fashion: Englishwomen's Dresses and their Construction c. 1860–1940.* London, Macmillan; Bradfield, N. (1968) *Costume in detail, Women's dress 1730–1930.* London, Macmillan. For sewing and stitches used at the turn of the 19th century, see de Dillmont, T. *Encyclopaedia of needlework.* Republished in 1987, London, Bracken Books.

Informative and inspiring high class photographs and drawing of costume details are found in Hart, A. and S. North (1998) *Historical Fashion in Detail. The 17th and 18th Centuries.* London, V & A Publications; Wilcox, C. and V. Mendes (1991) *Modern Fashion in Detail.* London, V & A Publications.

In this chapter, the following works have been used:

Andersen, E. (1977) *Danske Dragter. Moden i 1700-årene.* Copenhagen, Nationalmuseet.
Cock-Clausen, I. (1994) *Danske Dragter. Moden 1890–1920.* Copenhagen, Nationalmuseet.
Ginsburg, M. B. (1975) Fashion: an art 1900–1939. In *Fashion 1900–1939.* London, Idea Books International, 10–21.
Hammar, B. and P. Rasmussen (2001) *Kvinlig mode under två sekel.* Lund, Signum.
Tarrant, N. (1996) The art of construction. In *The Development of Costume.* Edinburgh, National Museum of Scotland, 104–135.
Waldén, L. *et al.* (1983) *Josefin och teknologin: tekniken sedd genom symaskinens nålsöga.* Stockholm, Sveriges Tekniska Museum.

Chapter 11

Ancient Female Costume: From Silent Cinema to Hollywood Glamour

Annette Borrell

Ever since the early days of cinema, historical dramas – better known as 'costume dramas' – have been a very popular film genre. This chapter will look at how classic film dramas represent ancient female costume from silent film to large-scale Hollywood productions of the 21st century. The author focuses on the aesthetic expression and costume styles of the leading ladies in classic ancient film dramas from a film history point of view, as their costumes generally represent the artistic high point of the film's costume designer. Historic dress in costume dramas always communicates a double message: on the one hand, an interpretation and reconstruction of the past, but on the other, a fashion statement on the dominating fashion of the era in which the film is produced.

Keywords: Hollywood, cinema, fashion, Roman, epic drama, identity, women.

In classic Hollywood publicity, it is often claimed that the reconstruction of the past and what is presented to the viewer on the screen is an authentic recreation of ancient life. However, all of Hollywood's directors, designers and publicity managers know and use historical films as marketing gimmicks to exploit film glamour. Scholars question to what extent 'historical' films reflect their contemporary societies, arguing how perception of the past is moulded by popular depictions of 'epic' history (Llewellyn-Jones 2005, 15). But to use the film medium as a platform for reconstructing costumes of the past is problematic, as the idea of historical precision collides with the aim of making lavish films with appeal to a mass audience. Within this field, an interesting discussion arises, as costumes of the characters seem more important to the film's narrative as a dramatic parameter than as an accurate reconstruction of historic dress.

After a brief introduction to film history, this chapter proceeds to unveil and describe the development of the representation of historic female costume from the early silent film drama *Nero – or the Fall of Rome* from 1909 to the large Oscar-winning Hollywood production *Gladiator* from 2000.

In textile research, one tends to work from a theory of the objective truth in terms of reconstructing the past. However, in film studies the premise is another. To discuss realism in a cinematic context is to examine the style of the film, for realism in this context is an aesthetic construction – a creation of style the filmmaker chooses for his film production. It relies on a set of rules or conventions mutually understood by the filmmaker and the viewer – a set of rules that the audience is capable of decoding (Branston and Stafford 2005). For instance, the presence of items such as togas and classical pillars immediately signal ancient film dramas.

THE COSTUME DRAMA AND THE COSTUME DESIGNER

The motion picture or cinema was created by the two French brothers, Auguste and Louis Lumière, in 1895. The first films were very simple in both form and style. They consisted only of short single shots framing action to show the sensational opportunities of the new motion picture. *Workers Leaving the Factory* and *A Train Arriving in the Station* are both films of short simple sequences by the Lumière brothers (Bordwell and Thompson 1993). Another Frenchman, George Méliès, created special effects and trick photography and is often credited as the actual creator of film fantasy or fiction (Branston and Stafford 2005). These early silent films did not emphasize leading ladies as happens later in film history. In the very beginning of film-making, set design and costumes did not have a high priority with the filmmaker and his audience. The actors merely wore contemporary clothes and only primitive props were used to emphasize the film's narrative.

Today costumes in film dramas play an important and central role for the total film experience. It is the costume designer who creates the right impression of the period in which the film is placed. Even though the costumes in epic dramas signal a specific period or 'period setting', this is not the only information they convey. For the contemporary fashion of the time in which the costumes were made left its trace in the costumes. These details that reveal the production time of the film are often difficult to discern for a contemporary audience. The past is viewed with the eyes of the present and the contemporary viewer is part of his or her own era and the dominating look of the age at the time a film is produced (Llewellyn-Jones 2005, 18).

The aim of costuming is to emphasize the character of a role. Often these costumes are not historically accurate, but act as messengers for the star-image of the lead female in the film. Yet, costume is also subjected to the budget and time schedule of a film production. The larger a budget for the film costumes, of course, the more possibilities exist for better and more thorough research and choice of different authentic materials for the costume designer. In cases of tight schedules, the costume designer is forced to compromise on his or her ambition of the overall look of a film's visual expression. For the costume designer, these criteria are sometimes even more burdensome if the film director decides to assert total control over the creative process and thus has veto rights over the costuming, as he or she often lacks the same knowledge and experience that the costume designer possesses within this field.

Hollywood film studios tend to base their work on the concept that epic dramas function as commercial channels exhibiting true Hollywood glamour. This factor is especially emphasized in relation to the personality and/or style of the leading female film roles.

According to Lloyd Llewellyn-Jones, costume design in classic film dramas often paint a rather conservative image of the ancient world. The perception of the past in epic film dramas is mostly based on visual rules and conventions of Victorian historical paintings from the 19th century and stage design from early 20th century theatre (Llewellyn-Jones 2005, 17). We can thus argue that the representation of the ancient world is based on visual clichés.

FEMALE COSTUMES IN THE FILM *NERO – OR THE FALL OF ROME*

Around 1909, there is a crucial change in film production, as 'set design' now becomes a growing and important contributory factor in the narrative of a film. *Nero – or the Fall of Rome* (1909) by Italian director Arturo Ambrosio is one of the first ancient dramas produced. Based on the story of the Roman emperor and tyrant Nero and the fire of Rome, this film is one of the first silent film productions to experiment with ancient costume. In both, duration and dimension, *Nero – or the Fall of Rome* was rather innovative in expression and style, and the film anticipates the revolutionary Italian epics, *The Last Days of Pompeii* (1913) and *Cabiria* (1914) that followed a few years later.

No costume designer is credited in *Nero – or the Fall of Rome*, and for the modern viewer, the set decoration resembles the static set decoration or tableau of theatre. However, for an early 20th century audience, the attempt to recreate days of old and to mime the ancient world was convincing (Llewellyn-Jones 2005). The female characters are not dressed in typical ancient Roman costume, but rather in dress inspired by ancient Greek sources. The costumes of the two female rivals, Poppea and Octavia, reflect historical dress rather superficially; yet the codes of the ancient world are recognizable to the viewer.

In *Nero,* it is easy to trace early 20th century fashion and style in both dresses and in the late-Victorian coiffures of the women. A further supporting female character in the film wears a typical early 20th century dress emphasizing waist and bosom, with long tight sleeves as contemporary fashion prescribes (see Ringgaard in this volume). And when Octavia is killed and falls to the ground she reveals a pair of typically Victorian high-heeled laced boots.

FEMALE COSTUMES IN THE FILM *INTOLERANCE*

D. W. Griffith – the renowned American film director of the early 20th century – was one of the first to produce costly and grandiose epic dramas. Today he still has a place in film history as one of the leading film-makers of his time (Bordwell and Thompson 1993). Griffith preferred the melodrama as the narrative form for his productions, a form which was particularly suitable for the genre of epic dramas. After the *Birth of a Nation* (1915), a pioneer production which set new standards for producing epic dramas, Griffith released *Intolerance* in 1916 – a masterpiece of its time. *Intolerance* is structured in four parallel stories – set in four different historical periods. In the original print, each story is tinted in different colours. Clare West, the costume designer of the film along with Griffith himself, was not credited. To make the impressive set design and costumes authentic to its era, Griffith closely studied the historical periods presented in the film. Yet, even so his story of *Babylon* (the biblical tale of the Fall of Babylon in 539 BC) describes his personal image of that city (Llewellyn-Jones 2005). However, it is important to note here that the settings still meet the visual conventions of an ancient setting of the cinema audience. What may have convinced the contemporary audience of *Intolerance* as realistic and true to historical sources seems highly stylized to a modern audience (Llewellyn-Jones 2005).

In the Babylonian story of *Intolerance,* one of the female leading ladies, the Mountain Girl played by Constance Talmadge, is dressed in rags. Her hair-style with its typical wavy pageboy cut and the characteristic make-up strongly indicate that the movie is produced in the early decades of the 20th century, thus giving the modern viewer information on how to decode fashion and style from around 1916**.** Seena Owen, as the Beloved Princess Attera in *Intolerance,* is one of the first actresses to display a 'historical' costume clearly inspired by fashion of that era. Dressed in a low-necked, chiffon dress with pearl embroidery, she resembles the glittery image in a modern fashion magazine. It is her headdress and heavy eye make-up that hint at ancient Babylonian costume.

The studios endeavoured to sell the idea that Hollywood actually undertook thorough research in recreating both ancient costumes and ancient locations. Furthermore, Hollywood studios claimed that what the audience viewed on the screen was authentic and faithful to historical detail.

THE ANCIENT WORLD AND FILM STAR GLAMOUR – FROM *CLEOPATRA* TO *GLADIATOR*

By the 1950s, costume drama was an established and a much used narrative form in film dramas. Joseph L. Mankiewicz was one of the prominent film directors of this period. In 1963, he directed the spectacular epic drama *Cleopatra,* featuring Elizabeth Taylor in the main role as Cleopatra, Queen of Ancient Egypt (69–30 BC). Irene Scharff is credited as costume designer in *Cleopatra*. At this time, it was rather common to let historical authenticity come second to design in the costumes of the female leading character. The look of Elizabeth Taylor's costumes in *Cleopatra* contains explicit sexual undertones. In several scenes she is displayed more or less undressed. The headdress and the characteristic eye make-up of Elizabeth Taylor's Cleopatra are inspired by ancient Egyptian iconography and recognizable to the audience, but the dresses she wears throughout the film are all in an undeniably 1960s style, having little to do with Egyptian dress but certainly making Elizabeth Taylor into a temptress (Fig. 11.1).

In this image (see Fig. 11.1), she is wearing a sleeveless dress with an explicit low-cut front, a marked waist and an accentuated bosom. Both the cut of the top of the dress and the material – a dark shimmery silky fabric and the pointed bosom are typical features for the 1950s and early 1960s actresses depicted as pin-up girls. On her right shoulder, a white scarf is draped. As mentioned earlier, the style of the hair-do and make-up of Elizabeth Taylor's Cleopatra are both inspired by ancient Egyptian iconography, but the overall look of the image is that of a stunningly beautiful construction. In classical film, the personality and style of the female star could never be subordinated to historical authenticity. Elizabeth Taylor's costumes of course had to suggest another time and place, but not at the expense of the glamorous film star image constructed around her figure by Hollywood studio publicity.

From the 1960s to the late 1990s, the ancient drama almost vanished as a narrative dramatic form in film. However, in 1996, screenwriter David Franzoni presented the story of what would become *Gladiator* (2000), directed by Ridley Scott, to DreamWorks. The tale of the Roman General Maximus takes place in AD 180. Maximus, played by Russell Crowe is deprived of his high rank and degraded to gladiator by the wicked Roman emperor Commodus. The story is fictional, but based on an actual moment in history. The main characters, the Roman emperor Marcus Aurelius (Richard Harris), Lucilla (his daughter, played by Connie Nielsen) and Emperor Commodus (Joaquin Phoenix) are all historical figures.

The makers of *Gladiator* intended to have powerful but contained acting, and not necessarily by well-known film stars. The choice of Danish-born actress Connie Nielsen is an example. Connie Nielsen was at the time a more or less blank page in Hollywood history. She is the main female character in *Gladiator*, but she does not attract the same distinctly sexual attention as Elizabeth Taylor did in *Cleopatra*. In *Gladiator*, both Lucilla and Maximus share the viewer's attention without directly exhibiting Lucilla as a pure sexual object. Nevertheless, Lucilla is the glamorous centre of the film. In an intelligent and low-key way, costume designer Janty Yates has managed to interpret and create her elegant and glamorous costumes. Janty Yates began her career in the fashion industry but switched careers into designing film costume. For *Gladiator*, she did extensive research to create the large set of costumes by studying books, galleries, museums and authentic jewellery in fashion at the time (Scott 2000).

In the opening sequence of *Gladiator*, Lucilla talks to Maximus after a battle in Germania. In this scene, Connie Nielsen wears an extravagant dark blue velvet robe edged with exquisite fur – presumably mink. Lucilla's gowns throughout the film are depicted as 'royal luxury' (www.fashion.at/film/glad31.htm), but the velvet in the robe she wears is not an ancient material nor is the look of the robe. The 21st-century look manifests itself in the choice of character for the role. Thus the choice of an unknown Connie Nielsen was intentional. She carries no previous Hollywood 'history' and therefore it is easier for the viewer to abstract from her as the actress Connie Nielsen and regard her as Lucilla. Nevertheless, she represents the look of a true Hollywood beauty with her fair skin, sensual lips, jewellery and natural worn hair.

Fig. 11.1: Elizabeth Taylor as Cleopatra (1963) (MPTV.NET)

In another sequence, Connie Nielsen/Lucilla talks to Richard Harris/Marcus Aurelius. They discuss the future of Rome. In this scene, she wears a dress with a ribbon strapped around her body from the bosom and down around the stomach and hips. The cleavage is deep and edged with lace. The material of the dress is softly draped on the body and looks different from for example Elizabeth Taylor's Cleoptara in her more sharp-cut typical 60's style. The softness in the draping of the fabric is characteristic for 21st century fashion design. This type of design is termed the 'Bohemian style' in contemporary fashion, with its natural materials, such as silk, cotton and linen. However, once again, the costumes are only loosely based on ancient Roman dress. The question is if film audiences twenty years hence would see these costumes as dating from the early 21st century?

Connie Nielsen's gowns were some of the most elaborate in the film. All the dresses were multilayered in luxurious materials like silk, satin, organza and chiffon. In all the scenes in which Connie Nielsen appears, she displays an overall glamorous look: on the one hand, she is a beautiful and powerful female character, but on the other, it is easy for the viewer to identify her as a scintillating Hollywood film star.

Janty Yates received an Oscar for her exquisite glamorous costume design in *Gladiator*. Costume design has come a long way since the early days of film-making when designers went unaccredited.

CONCLUSIONS

Since the time of early silent film dramas, costume has played an important role, and already in *Intolerance* from 1916, an increased stylish and glamorous focus on the female leading characters was settled. Hollywood studios claim to strive for historical accuracy when reconstructing the past in epic dramas, but in describing the past the screenwriter at the same time writes about his or her world. From the early epic drama *Nero – or the Fall of Rome,* to the recent ancient epic drama *Gladiator,* leading ladies have always made a fashion statement to the viewer, and thus reflected the world in which the film was made.

The interaction between popular culture and historical representation has become an accepted area of academic debate. Scholars question whether historical dramas actually reflect the societies, which they depict. The ancient costumes of the female characters seem more important to the film's narrative as a dramatic parameter than as an accurate reconstruction of ancient Egyptian or Roman dress. The epic costume dramas are created from an interpretation of history – an interpretation with which the audience is able to identify itself. Using beautiful and glamorous female leading characters, costume dramas reflect contemporary fashion and aesthetics.

ACKNOWLEDGEMENTS

I would like to thank costume designer Pernille Egeskov Bigum for her research help; Karen Lund Petersen (Copenhagen University), Henning Pryds (University of Southern Denmark) and Christa Lykke Christensen (Copenhagen University) for reading the manuscript and making valuable comments.

BIBLIOGRAPHY

Bordwell, D. and K. Thompson (1993) *Film Art – An Introduction,* 4th ed., McGraw-Hill, University of Wisconsin.

Branston, G. and R. Stafford (2005) *The Media Student's Book*. 3rd ed., London, Routledge.

Llewellyn-Jones, L. (2005) The Fashioning of Delilah. Costume Design, Historicism and Fantasy in Cecil B. DeMille's *Samson and Delilah* (1949). In L. Cleland, M. Harlow and Llewellyn-Jones (eds) *The Clothed Body in the Ancient World*. Oxford, Oxbow Books, 14–29.

Scott, R. (2000) Introduction. In Landau, D. (ed.) *Gladiator – The Making of the Ridley Scott Epic*. New York, Newmarket Press & DreamWorks and Universal Studios.

Wilson, E. (1985) *Adorned in Dreams*. I. B. Tauris & Co. Ltd, Denmark.

FILMS

Nero – or the Fall of Rome (1909). Directed by Arturo Ambrosio.

Intolerance (1916). Directed by D. W. Griffith.

Cleopatra (1963). Directed by Joseph L. Mankiewicz.

Gladiator (2000). Directed by Ridley Scott.

WEBSITE

www.fashion.at/film/glad31.htm
This site also includes Connie Nielsen's costumes in *Gladiator* discussed in this article.

2000 BC   1000 BC   AD 1   AD 500

AD 1000   AD 1500   AD 2000

Created by Agnete Wisti Lassen